GOTTFRIED TRITTEN

ART TECHNIQUES FOR CHILDREN

GOTTFRIED TRITTEN

Art Techniques
for Children

 REINHOLD PUBLISHING CORPORATION · NEW YORK

Originally published in Switzerland as "Gestaltende Kinderhände"
© 1959 by Paul Haupt Berne

Introduction

When children express themselves pictorially, they try to conquer reality. Techniques and materials are only a means to fulfill this aim.

This book does not follow any particular educational philosophy. It deals mainly with techniques and materials in order to help children stay away from formulas. The use of the techniques has meaning only if it helps to awaken the child's creativity. The selection of techniques and materials justifies itself only if it increases expressiveness, thereby freeing and developing the personality.

The book is directed to teachers in elementary schools and kindergarten. Parents interested in participating in their children's development will also find it useful. All the examples are done by students during school hours.

I am fully aware of the limitations of the book. It makes no claim of universal appeal, but if it can make a contribution toward an awareness of art, it will fulfill its purpose.

I thank my wife and all others who have helped to make this book possible.

Thun, Switzerland
Summer 1958

Gottfried Tritten

Contents

* This survey follows in its main outlines **150 Techniques in Art** by Hans Meyers, published in 1963 by Reinhold Publishing Corporation.

In the exercises the letter "G" after one of the "Similar Subjects" indicates a group project.

ART TECHNIQUES FOR CHILDREN

Aims

I. Experience and Imagination

Up to the age of eleven, children create entirely from imagination. The development of the imagination is therefore one of the chief concerns of creative art and craft teaching.

Imagination is based on experience. Children hunger for experience because they need to adapt themselves to their surroundings. They long to master reality. The accumulation of experience within them urges children towards expression.

Experience is gained both from inside and outside the personality. It is our task to increase the ability to gain experience, to bring order and meaning into it, and to allow experiences to crystallize into clear and distinct images. The development of the imagination also brings with it an increased sensitivity. Understanding widens, and other faculties, such as the aesthetic sense and the powers of observation, memory, thought, and fantasy, are strengthened in consequence.

The child's mode of expression changes constantly throughout the stages of his development. This fact is of the utmost importance in the choice of projects.

II. The Creative Process

Imagination demands to be given form. We call this the creative urge. It is our task to help the child towards a strong creative urge and towards individual expression. Nothing must interfere with the originality of the work. We must guide in such a way that the transformation of experience into visible form—*i.e.*, the creative process—becomes conscious. This is as much an inner as an outer activity, and the visible results are not the only ones that matter. The aim must be vitality and independence. The importance of the technique must not be underrated in this connection. Though technique and materials are only means to an end, mastery of them will greatly affect the result. By making a child familiar with a technique, we help him to develop his imagination and to acquire confidence, the ability to concentrate, and pleasure in his work.

A. The Importance of the Subject

It is not enough to choose some obvious subject and let children start work without any preliminaries. The subject must be the key to the child's interior world; it must fire his imagination for there to be any real success. Every theme must therefore come from the realm of the child's own experience. To put a subject on paper can never be an end in itself; the real purpose must be to give form to part of the child's experience. In drawing, the child tells us what he has learned from reality and his attitude to it. He rarely deals with a subject in isolation. Everything is part of a wider experience. Real and unreal mingle; the accidental falls away, and the essential comes to the fore.

The teacher must allow for these relationships in the choice of subject. It would not be right to give "the cat" as a task, but "our cat"; not "the cornfield" but "gathering corn"; not "the giant" but "David and Goliath."

Subjects have been chosen at random throughout this book. Certain ones were selected because they seemed to demonstrate a technique particularly well. It is up to the teacher to bring the subject into a living relationship with the child's experience. This book merely offers a framework within which the widest variations are possible.

In the first year of school, the principal subjects are human beings, houses, animals, and plants.

The first relationship the child establishes is with other human beings. He therefore represents himself and those closest to him—his mother, father, brothers and sisters, and friends. Children hardly ever produce any drawings that do not contain people. The child tells of them, places them within his experience, shows sympathy and antipathy. In all simplicity, he knows how to depict essential characteristics. The relationship of head and body, the position of the legs, as well as gestures and attitudes, are entirely characteristic and indicate far more than external features. At the age of seven children prefer a view from the front; later, we find the profile, and with it movement and action.

At first, the child experiences animals as if they were human beings; he talks to them and endows them with feelings and expression. Good and wicked animals can be the subject of conflict. The child senses the character of an animal at once and gives it its basic qualities. Animals provide valuable subjects. In drawing and painting they frequently appear in profile, except for the head, wich is often shown from the front.

The house also is an important subject in the early years of school life. It represents shelter and protection, the safe island from which the child sets out for the gradual conquest of the world. Spatial renderings of houses are possible from the age of seven on. But usually children of seven will show only one façade, later two, or even three, all on the same base. Perspective drawings must not under any circumstances be attempted too early. With the increasing experience of space, the child's interest in perspective will develop on its own. Among the plant kingdom, trees occupy an important place in children's drawings. Flowers are experienced very intensely, but grasses are too abstract and remote for the child of that age.

B. The Sense of Form

The child usually possesses an unconscious, yet absolutely sure, sense of form. He has an instinctive feeling for the nature of an object, for the contrasts of form, color, technique, and material. However, despite the child's certainty in these matters, we cannot simply allow him a free hand. It is the author's view that here, too, gentle guidance is possible, since the development of the creative faculty runs parallel to the unfolding of intelligence and experience.

Each phase of development, and its related experience of the world, gives us a starting point for setting tasks. Thus the typically linear experience of the child between five and seven calls for a development of his feeling for outline through exercises with pencil, pen, brush, paper, and wire.

12

Gradually, the child will advance from the line to the plane. Expansion, proportion, the distribution of areas, quantity, and order are by no means problems of which the child is unaware, though he will not experience them consciously.

The tactile stage in the small child's experience of the world accompanies the development of the sense of touch; it is greatly helped by modeling of every kind.

The experience of form and space calls for tasks involving intersecting planes; it leads on to the beginnings of parallel perspective.

C. The Sense of Color

Children use color expressively rather than naturalistically. An object is judged according to its character and given the color appropriate to it. The emotional rather than the aesthetic quality of the color is decisive.

Sooner or later, color is used in a more naturalistic way. Grass becomes green, tree trunks brown, the sky blue, the sun yellow. The child is not aware of background. Even placing an object into the colors of its surroundings can be a new experience for the child of seven and must therefore be attempted gradually.

What is our aim in training the sense of color? Whatever way colors are used, whether expressively or naturalistically, the feeling for color can, and indeed must, be developed. We quite consciously set tasks involving contrasting colors (light-dark, cold-warm, complementary, etc.). Exercises of this kind by themselves will produce the desired result, without ever telling the child a word about color theories.

D. The Feeling for Materials

The experience of the material is a great delight to the child and should therefore be encouraged. This is not merely a question of training the sense of touch, but above all of experiencing the very character of an object. The possibility of combining materials must be exploited to the utmost, whether we are looking for an appropriate subject for each material or choosing the material for a particular subject.

E. The Feeling for Ornament and Decoration

The feeling for ornament should be developed in the early years of school. It can begin with the decoration of simple objects. Ornament does not exist on its own, but is an important addition, giving the object it decorates articulation, even splendor, and increased significance. Every type of ornament consists of one or several motifs. These can be arranged in different ways—either lined up, over an area, or in scatter designs.

By way of suggestion, several motifs suitable for younger children are shown on the following page.

F. Further Considerations

Like any other subject, the teaching of art in all its aspects forms part of the general curriculum. It will be one-sided, and even misplaced, if it does not constantly aim at the development of the whole personality.

Visual Experience. The aim is to teach the child to look and observe.

Liberation. Like play, dance, or music, our type of art teaching aims at liberating the child. Misplaced or dormant faculties are guided along the right path. Such liberation is bound to help a child's entire education.

Discipline. A carefully formulated task and a clearly outlined working process allow the child to concentrate. Absent-minded, restless, or overexuberant children can only benefit from quiet yet imaginative work.

Aesthetic Experience. It may seem premature to speak at this early stage of development of the aesthetic sense. Certainly, no direct attempts must be made to develop the critical faculty in small children. It should grow entirely out of the way the lesson is given. If art is properly taught, the feeling for what is good and bad will come by itself. Aesthetics will have been taught subconsciously, without wasting a single word on it, for it is not the visual-aesthetic problem that is decisive to the child, but the harmony of creative expression and inner vision.

Skill. Manual skills must not be neglected. Apart from purely practical considerations, they form part of a complete education. It is advisable, therefore, to let the child occasionally use both hands simultaneously, or even only the left.

G. Looking at Works of Art

Whether the child's attention should be drawn to works of art, very much depends on the way this is done. Children should undoubtedly be shown sculptures and paintings. These may even serve as a source of inspiration in their practical work. But attempts to have them analyze art or, worse still, copy it, would be quite wrong. Works of art are experienced like picture books and should be looked at in the same way. This is a preparation for a truly aesthetic approach in later years.

III. Methods

A. Basic Principles

Preparation

The best preparation for producing creative work is to be quite clear about the aim. What is wanted? How can it be produced? Regarding technique, it is advisable that the teacher work out every task himself. He will thus become aware of the problems that may arise and will not overrate them. It will therefore help considerably if each step is planned in advance.

Guidance

1. Working from Imagination. Since younger children work chiefly from imagination, it is important to cultivate the individual character of both imagination and expression. The directness and originality of childhood should be preserved as far as possible. The naturally naïve approach must not be suppressed, though it should not be exploited. Imagination can be combined with observation.

2. Working from Memory and Observation. This method is used increasingly after the age of eight. Here, progress comes in spurts rather than gradually. Through discussion and observation of the object in question, experience becomes more intense and imagination widens.

It is important not to copy. Children must always work from memory, never from nature. But, although attention is limited to the basic essentials of an object when children are working from imagination, greater attention is given to detail when they are working from memory and observation. Experience becomes more conscious. The basis of observation is always the object itself.

As children grow older, a more detailed observation is encouraged. Here, too, individuality and directness must not be destroyed.

3. Working from Nature. This method is unsuitable for younger children.

Assessing Work

When judging work, the teacher must not have any preconceived ideas about results. Instead, he should try to develop a sense of the specific quality of each example. He must not judge by naturalistic standards. The term "correct" is relative and should be based entirely on the intellectual and manual capacities of each child.

B. Two Examples

1. Working from Imagination

This project is suitable for children aged eight.

Subject: A cockerel.
Technique: Limited range of poster colors.
Materials: Bright yellow paper, about 16 inches by 12 inches; red and black poster colors; bristle and sable brush; water container; palette; sponge; old newspapers.
Time: Two hours.

a) Experience and Imagination

Where the imagination is intense, there is no need to stimulate it; otherwise the image has to be built up with a description of a cockerel—for example, he raises his head, opens his sharp beak and crows; he flaps his wings and his curved tail feathers flutter in the breeze. It is important to keep the whole picture in mind, for it is that which corresponds to the child's imagination and gives the child's work its monumental and convincing quality.

Drawings on the blackboard, photographs, and reproductions of pictures can be of great help. Properly used, they will strengthen the imagination. Wrongly used, such as at the beginning of a lesson, they can weaken imagination and originality.

The introductory talk should be short—ten minutes is quite sufficient.

b) The Creative Process

Technique. This subject cannot be discussed often enough. A demonstration is the simplest, shortest, and most effective way to teach technique.

In our example, we introduce the drawing of lines with the brush, the structural effect of the brushwork (feathers), the darkening of red with black, and the method of letting patches of the paper show through. The child should be left as much freedom as possible. The paper should be upright; the cockerel must fill the entire sheet. (With individual objects, some indication of size generally proves helpful.)

Control. Children should work independently and with as little interruption as possible. Suggestions about form, color, technique, etc., are quite permissible, always bearing in mind each child's individual approach. It would be very wrong to try to force one's own conceptions about the subject into the child's work.

2. Working from Memory and Observation

This project is suitable for 11-year-olds.

Theme: A dahlia.

Technique: Wax crayons.

Materials: White cartridge paper, not too coarse-grained, about 16 inches by 12 inches; pencil; rubber; wax crayons; dahlias.

Time: Four hours.

The work is organized in several stages, during each of which the dahlias are first observed and then put aside. The children work from memory, supplemented by observation.

Stage 1

Study of Form. If at all possible, the children should look at a whole dahlia plant in the garden. The stalks are firm and almost vertical. Some of the smaller stalks are straight, others are curved. The alternation between curved and straight lines provides tension and rhythm.

The flowers, seen from above, are circular; sideways, they appear as semicircles. The lanceolate petals are grouped in layers and radiate outwards. The outer ones are bigger than the inner ones, and the flowers themselves are of different sizes.

The buds resemble small bells; the sepals are pointed.

The leaves, largest and heaviest near the base, occur singly and in groups. They are broad and pointed, with serrated edges.

Representation from Imagination and Memory. The children should use the smooth side of the paper, which is upright. The dahlia is sketched in outline in pencil. Suggestions about form, distribution, proportion, etc., are permissible. This stage takes about an hour.

Stage 2

Consideration of Color. The observation of color should increase in importance with age. The stalks are a light yellowish green. To make them stand out more on the white paper, they can be placed against darker leaves. Different shades of green should be used: light green (with yellow), pale green (with white and blue), olive green (with white and brown).

The blooms should be in various radiant colors, such as reddish purple, crimson, purple, bright red, salmon pink, violet, blood red.

The sepals should be dark green and the buds the same color as the flowers.

Leaves ought to be in greens different from the green of the stalks, the leaves rather less intense than the stalks; they form a contrast to the brilliant blooms. Light-colored flowers can be shown against a darker background.

Technique. Pencil lines are, as far as possible, erased with a rubber. The wax crayon technique needs no further explanation. The teacher should briefly mention ways of mixing color (see page 62) and scraping techniques.

Representation from Imagination and Memory. Some children will tend to work more out from imagination, others more from memory. Again, suggestions regarding color, technique, etc., are quite permissible. This stage should last about two and a half hours.

Stage 3

Discussion. It is advisable to display the complete drawings on the wall and to discuss them. In one case, the use of bright colors will appear particularly good, in another the gradation of the colors, in a third the use of contrasting forms, in a fourth the accurate observation, in a fifth the general impression, etc. This stage should take about half an hour.

IV. Tools and Materials

It is important that the pupil work on a cardboard base. Chip board, or hardboard, about 14 inches by 16 inches, will serve this purpose. Ordinary pencils, colored pencils, wax crayons, and a sponge are also necessary.

The art room should have the following basic equipment:

Sticks of charcoal
Fixative and fixative spray
Brushes—sable and flat bristle
Pencil sharpener
Water bowls
Palettes
Clothes pegs
Poster colors
Scissors
Old razor blades (with holders, or cutting tool)
Sieve
Old toothbrushes
Lino-cutting tools (one per pupil) and sharpener
Spatulas (about five per class)
Rubber rollers
Modeling tools (one per pupil)

Clay box (tin-lined)
Plaster box (wood, lined for waterproofing if possible)
Tin shears
Hammers (several)
Flat-nosed pliers (several)
Sharp-nosed pliers (several)
Sheet of glass, about 28 inches by 28 inches, or several about 12 inches by 8 inches
Newsprint, cartridge paper, gray and white drawing paper, wrapping paper,
    colored paper for painting and cutting out.

V. Techniques

New techniques or materials present few problems to smaller children; they are concerned simply with describing in a different way with different means. It is not a question of merely trying out new techniques, but of adapting them to the child's urge for expression and of developing and perfecting them accordingly. To achieve some degree of technical mastery it is advisable to work in the same technique for between two and eight consecutive lessons, so that its possibilities can be demonstrated and evolved independently.

A. Drawing Techniques

Pencil Drawing

We use the narrative line drawing throughout the primary school. The possibilities of this technique should be demonstrated and fully exploited. Lines, areas, and surface textures can all be drawn in pencil. Strong linear exercises are more suitable for the first two years at school, other techniques for slightly older children. The spontaneously drawn line has a charm of its own and should therefore never be redrawn or traced. Strokes should be bold. Pencil drawing is suitable for designing and sketching, as well as for descriptive illustrations. Pencils of any degree of hardness can be used, though 3 B or 4 B will be found most suitable. 7 B is the softest, 9 H the hardest, pencil. HB is a medium-hard pencil. A rubber eraser—and always a soft one—should be used only for very bad mistakes.

Pencil Drawing I. A Fairy-Tale Castle

Materials   2B, 3B, and 4B pencils, sheet of white drawing paper, about 14 inches by 10 inches.

Subject   The fairy-tale castle is shown in cross section. All the rooms, staircases, furnishings, and people can be seen. A view of this kind corresponds to the child's imagination. There is no need to adhere to the cross section too literally.

The castle is briefly explained to the children, the different parts—walls, towers, battlements, gateways, the interior with stairs, great hall, kitchen, and corridors—being pointed out. Nor are furniture (tables, chairs, wardrobes, etc.) and inhabitants forgotten.

Technique   The technical possibilities of pencil drawing should be demonstrated. More delicate lines will require a hard pencil, thick black lines a soft one. Different degrees of pressure will produce a lighter or darker, a thinner or thicker, line. The castle should fill the entire sheet. A vertical format is probably preferable. The smooth side of the paper should be used.

The drawing shown in our illustration was done in the first grade (six to seven years).

Similar subjects: monkey / ant / apple tree / Noah's ark / at the doctor / along the stream / bakery / station / building site / farmyard / bee / botanical gardens / castle / Tom Thumb / thistle / cathedral / village / village band / Sleeping Beauty / dragon / lizard / railway / angel / Eskimo / factory / bicycle / family at table / fern / carnival procession / at the window / holiday episode / fire brigade / fish / fisherman / fishing port / escape / airplane / football teams / galley / birthday / Puss in Boots / giraffe / city / harbor / cock / my dream house / plan of a house / house building / household utensils / harvest time / grasshopper / stag / shepherd and his flock / skyscraper / wedding / woodcutter / chicken house / dog / Red Indian / insects / instruments / the hunt / fun fair / jazz band / cage with birds or animals / battle of the knights / merry-go-round / cat / church / the three wise men from the East / crane / crocodile / coach / teacher / dragonfly / hobby / lion hunt / dandelion / market / machines / bricklayer / military inspection / sea gull / nightingale / rhinoceros / Neptune / hippopotamus / oasis / orchestra / ornament / palace / desert island / paradise / lake dwelling / the Trojan Horse / at the photographer's / pirate ship / racing cyclists / caterpillar / the day of departure / giant / knight / Robinson Crusoe / Little Red Ridinghood / ship / sleep / blacksmith / snail / Snow White and the Seven Dwarfs / joiner / shoemaker / schoolroom / sea horse / tightrope-walker / self-portrait / skier / soldiers / sunflower / spider / sportsman / Santa Claus / town / walking on stilts / design for embroidery / bull / stork / on the beach / train / in the room / dancer / tug of war / William Tell / theater / at the table / magic table / dream / gym lesson / flood / jungle / my favorite occupation / traffic signals / cattle market / bird's nest / animals of the wood / Christmas tree / wharf / tools / sports competition / goblin / windmill / robot / at the dentist / magician / magic wood / camping ground / goat / gypsy / carpenter / circus / zoo / dwarf.

Pencil Drawing II. Our House

Materials   Same as in the first exercise, using light-gray wrapping paper, about 10 inches by 8 inches, lengthwise.

Subject   The lesson begins with a short introductory talk pointing out the main features of a house.

Technique   Here, in contrast to the previous exercise, the emphasis is on the plane rather than the line. The scale from black to white allows an almost unlimited variety of shades, though adjoining areas should form contrasts. Shading over one area should follow the same direction and should be fairly even.

The main object of interest is the house, which is first lightly drawn in outline. The different portions are then filled in, taking care to make adjoining areas contrast. Even empty spaces create their own effect.

The drawing shown in our illustration was done in the second grade (seven to eight years).

Similar Subjects: ant / blackbird / apple tree / aquarium / Noah's ark / slums / car / station / balloon seller / building site / blackberry / well / castle / clown / village / dragon design / railway / icebergs / elephant / jackdaw / duck / donkey / industrial town / fish in a net / fishing port / flamingo / escape / goose / a journey by gondola / galleys / city / cock / house building / a witch's house / gates of heaven / skyscraper / bride and bridegroom / chicken house / bumblebee / wigwam / initials / beetle / camel / chimney sweep / rabbit / cat / centaur / pebbles / crane / crab / cow / leopard / lion / dandelion / locomotive / ladybird / mask / mouse / man in the moon / rhinoceros / hippopotamus / ornament / palace / panther / parrot / peacock / at the photographer's / pirate ship / rainy day / boa constrictor / knight / Robinson Crusoe / flock of sheep / tortoise / snake / butterfly / story of the creation / shoemaker / school building / pig / soldiers / Santa Claus / town / bull / pansy / the street in which I live / room / my valley / pine wood / pigeon / carpet / devil / deep sea diver / wood / wood hut / washing day / design for weaving / wild duck / winter landscape / wolf / cloud / dream house / at the dentist / zebra / goat / circus tent.

Pencil Drawing III. Wild Man of the Mountain

Materials Same as in the first exercise, using gray paper, about 14 inches by 6 inches.

Subject The lesson begins with a short introductory talk about the character and appearance of the Wild Man of the Mountain—a giant with small head, unkempt hair, long beard and drooping mustache, savage eyes, huge hands, dressed in skins, with a tree trunk for his stick.

Technique Here, the children experiment with texture: dots (for the hair on arms and legs, or the pattern of his trousers), short strokes (for his beard or the skins he wears), scrolls (for his hair), a regular pattern (for his smock, sack, etc.).
The texture should be flat, rather than three-dimensional. It enlivens the surface and expresses the specific quality of various materials such as fur, hair, bark, etc.
The Wild Man of the Mountain is a giant and should occupy the entire page. It is important that the children work from their free imagination.

The drawing shown in our illustration was done in the third grade (eight to nine years).

Similar Subjects: monkey / ant / aster / bear / buffalo / clown / dahlia / demon / David and Goliath / dragon / oak / squirrel / polar bear / duck / owl / pheasant / bat / goose / vegetable market / giraffe / Puss in Boots / cock / hamster / harlequin / peddler / harvest time / stag / shepherd and his flock / woodcutter / hen / dog / hedgehog / huntsman / cacti / camel / animal fight / rabbit / cat / screech owl / crocodile / cow / leopard / lion / corn-cob / men from Mars / mouse / nightingale / oasis / parrot / bird of paradise / lake dwelling / peacock / pirate / robber / caterpillar / rain / reindeer / Robinson Crusoe / sheep / jewelry / snail shell / tailor / story of creation / sunflower / Santa Claus / design for embroidery / bull / fir tree / pigeon / carpet / devil / tropical island / monster / jungle / cattle market / birds / bird's nest / Christmas tree / goblin / ram / weasel / wolf / magic bird / goat / gypsy / circus / zoo / dwarf.

Pencil Drawing IV. Fir Tree

Materials   Same as in the first exercise, using light-brown, or possibly light-blue, paper, about 14 inches by 10 inches, lengthwise.

Subject   The lesson begins with a short introductory talk about the fir tree, either with the help of a drawing on the blackboard, or while looking at a real tree (see page 17). There are certain important features, such as the trunk tapering towards the top and the different directions of the branches (pointing downward at the bottom, horizontal in the middle, and upward at the top), which must not be ignored.

Technique   Here, the different ways (line, plane, texture) of pencil drawing are combined. The tree should fill the whole page. Though the outline sketch must not be too rigid, the drawing should be carefully worked out.

The drawing shown in our illustration was done in the fourth grade (nine to ten years). Because of its more detailed treatment, the theme does not lend itself very well for use with younger children.

Similar Subjects: switchback / monkey / ant / blackbird / apple tree / aquarium / Noah's ark / the arctic regions / artist / Cinderella / car / river bed / baker and bakery / station / building site / farmyard / beehive / at the well / clown / Tom Thumb / David and Goliath / cathedral / village band / Sleeping Beauty / dragon / oak / lizard / railway / icebergs / duck / donkey / Eskimo camp / owl / factory / family / fern / holiday / fish haul / escape / football match / galley / the goose girl / garden / birthday party / Puss in Boots / herd of giraffes / a journey by gondola / city / cock / harlequin / house building / peddler / witch / witch hut / shepherd and his flock / the construction of a skyscraper / wedding coach / woodcutter / bumblebee / dog / Indian chief / insects / the hunt / huntsman / fun fair / Joseph and Mary / jeweler / cage with animals / a merry-go-round / cat / in the shop / screech owl / crocodile / flight of cranes / teacher and his pupils / hobby / lion hunt / locomotive / rabble / ladybird / market day / man from Mars / bricklayer / ocean bed / military inspection / church / musical instruments / nightingale / rhinoceros / Neptune / hippopotamus / oasis / fruit-picking / orchestra / palace / desert island / Garden of Eden / horse-racing / at the photographer's / mushrooms / pirate ship / robbers / rainy weather / episode on a journey / rider / reindeer / giant / knight / Robinson Crusoe / Little Red Ridinghood / flock of sheep / in front of a shop window / ship / tortoise / sleep / snake / castle / blacksmith / snail / Snow White and the Seven Dwarfs / tailor / story of creation / shoemaker / shoes / educational trip / swimming / sea horse / sailing yacht / tightrope-walker / self-portrait / skier / soldiers / summer / sunflower / spider / sportsman / Santa Claus / town / walking on stilts / bull / stork / on the beach / tram / room / heavy gale / dancer / pigeon / William Tell / carpet / devil / theater / deep sea diver / at the table / dream / tropical island / gym lesson / moving house / monster / jungle / my favorite occupation / traffic / cattle market / scarecrow / wood / the house in the wood / Christmas / wharf / goblins / wild duck / winter / magic bird / magician / magic wood / circus / zoo / dwarf.

Pen Drawing

Pen drawing can be attempted even with younger children. Indeed, it forms a particularly good introduction to writing with pen and ink. In the first two years of school, the emphasis will be more on line, in the third and fourth year, on both line and texture.

The children must always draw directly, and not trace pencil sketches, if their work is to retain its spontaneity.

Reed pens, goose quills, sticks of wood, and even matches—as well as pens of every kind—should be experimented with. Ink or drawing ink should be of good quality; the paper—not necessarily white—should be smooth or absorbent.

Pen drawing can be attempted in the first grade; from the second grade onward, it should be a regular subject.

Pen Drawing I. Line Drawing: Magic Flower, or Carpet Design

Materials Drawing pens of different widths; penholder; rags; drawing ink; smooth white paper, about 8 inches by 8 inches; blotting paper.

Subject We begin with a point at the center of the page, around which we arrange motif after motif to form a magic flower or a carpet (round or square).

Technique The teacher should demonstrate the correct use of the pen where necessary.
The possibilities of line drawing (thin or wide, long or short) should be demonstrated, giving several examples of simple designs on the blackboard (see page 14). Larger shapes can be filled with smaler motifs. It is important to work slowly and carefully.

This work was made in the second grade (seven to eight years), when pen and ink were first introduced.

Similar Subjects: apple tree / aquarium / Noah's ark / aster / bed of a stream / dredger / house plan / broom-maker / wreath of flowers / dahlia / cathedral / the palace of Sleeping Beauty / dragon / lizard / angel / duck / strawberry / Eskimo / bicycle / fish / bat / airplane / frog / goose / Puss in Boots / cock / hamster / chicken / hedgehog / Indian / insects / red currant / necklace / cage with birds / cathedral / screech owl / crane / crocodile / bookmark / corncob / sea gull / church / marmot / musical instruments / mask / nightingale / carnations / ornament / palace / mushroom / palm tree / caterpillar / rainy weather / bowling / a hoop / rhythmical exercises / boa constrictor / Robinson Crusoe / tortoise / snake / butterfly / jewelry / snail shell / swan / pig / swimming / sea horse / sunflower / spider's web / town / design for embroidery / fir tree / carpet / devil / place cards / tiger / tropical island / jungle / bird's nest / wood / design for weaving / Christmas tree / tools / windmill / wolf / skyscraper / robot / dream house / magic wood / goat / dwarf.

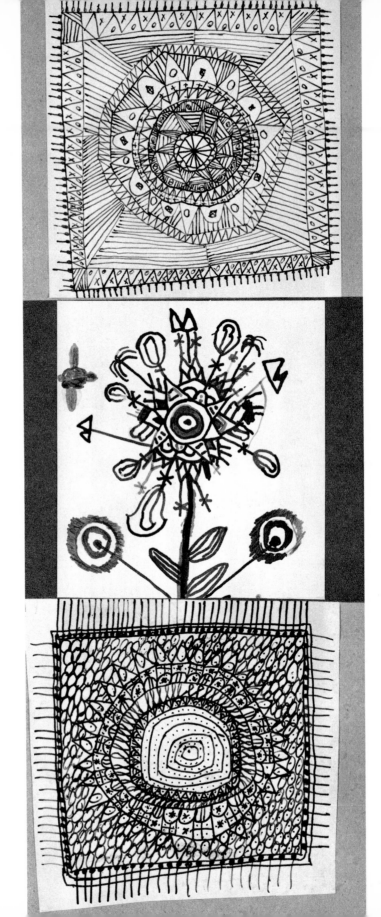

Pen Drawing II. Free Use of the Line: A Railway

Materials $^1/_{16}$-inch nib; penholder; rag and blotting paper; smooth nonabsorbent paper (white or pale yellow), about 16 inches by 4 inches; drawing ink.

Subject   The lesson begins with a short introductory talk. The train consists of a locomotive (steam or electric) and the cars attached to it. The younger child experiences the sound and movement of the train rather than its external characteristics.

A sketch on the blackboard gives some idea of the basic form: rails with stones in between, wheels on the rails, and above these railroad cars with roof, windows, steps, and doors. Each car has buffers and an inscription.

Technique   In the first grade, the children will not yet be acquainted with pen and ink, the use of which will therefore have to be demonstrated. Lines must be drawn in long strokes, not in spurts. It is advisable to work from right to left.

This drawing was made in the first grade (six to seven years). The subject is also suitable for third- and fourth-grade children; with them the drawing should be based on observation (see page 17).

Similar Subjects: switchback / monkey / angler / apple harvest / aquarium / the building of Noah's ark / cross section of Noah's ark / at the doctor / auto racing / beach scene / station / building site / beehive / botanical gardens / at the well / castle / clown / tiler / David and Goliath / village / oak forest / a squirrel / in a pine wood / lizard / ice hockey / a choir of angels / Eskimos on the move / factory / pheasants fighting / holiday episode / spotted salamander / thimble / haul of fish / flamingo / escape / footballer / galley / the goose girl / garden / vegetable woman / Puss in Boots / trip in a gondola / city / harbor / harlequin / witch / a witch's house / stag / shepherds with their flocks / house building / plan of a house / wedding procession / woodcutter / chicken house / dog / attack by Indians / the hunt / fun fair / beetle / cage / camel ride / merry-go-round / chervil / church / three wise men from the East / teacher and pupils / favorite occupation / dandelion / locomotive / swing / rabble / market day / marten / men from Mars / machines / ocean bed / military inspection / hippopotamus / oasis / fruit picking / orchestra / lake dwelling / peacock / Trojan Horse / pirate ship / cycle racing / day of departure / rider / reindeer / Robinson Crusoe / Little Red Ridinghood / a flock of sheep / in front of a shop window / ship / me asleep / palace / blacksmith / snails / Snow White and the Seven Dwarfs / tailor / the story of creation / joiner / shoemaker / educational trip / swimming / sailboat / tightrope-walker / self-portrait / ski lift / skier / soldiers / sportsmen / at the seashore / trolley / dance / tug of war / William Tell / theater / deep sea diver / at the table / dream / tropical island / gymnast / house moving / jungle / my favorite occupation / traffic / cattle market / forest / Christmas / wharf / competition / the goblins / windmill / The Wolf and the Seven Kids / skyscraper / desert journey / robot / dream wish / quarrel / magician / news vendor / camping site / goatsherd / gypsy / circus / dwarf.

Pen Drawing III. Combining Line and Texture: Snakes

Materials   Two pens, one very pointed, the other $1/16$ inch wide, reed pen or goose quill; ink or drawing ink; penholder; rag and blotting paper; absorbent paper, 12 inches by 12 inches (newsprint).

Subject   The lesson begins with a short introductory talk. We draw a group of coiled-up snakes, each with a different marking.
One snake forms the beginning; it winds its way across the paper. After first being drawn in outline, it is then decorated with a repetitive design. The next snake is decorated differently, as is a third and, possibly, a fourth. Any confusion between the snakes, because of similarity of their designs, must be avoided.

Technique   It should be demonstrated to the children that the pen can not only draw lines, but can also create the effect of texture by means of dots, patches, short strokes, or patterns.
When absorbent paper is used, the pen must not be allowed to linger.

This drawing was done in the t h i r d grade (eight to nine years). One snake would be enough in the first year.

Similar Subjects: artist / bed of a stream with varicolored pebbles / building materials / chameleon / clown / dragon / lizard / jackdaw / fish / frog / football team / garden / birthday cake / harlequin / a witch's house / gates of heaven / Indians / initials / jaguar / necklace / beetle / calendar leaf / pebbles / leopards / bookmark / ornaments / Venetian or Oriental palace / peacock / mushrooms / caterpillar / boa constrictor / tortoise / butterfly / jewelry / snail shell / design for embroidery / timetable / carpet / place cards / tiger / gymnast / jungle / traffic sign / design for weaving / Christmas tree / goblins / skyscraper / robot / camping ground / a flock of goats / circus folk / in the zoo / dwarf.

Pen Drawing IV. Ghosts

Materials Thin nib pen, possibly reed; penholder; ink or drawing ink; rag and blotting paper; smooth pale-gray paper, about 14 inches by 10 inches.

Subject What is a ghost? A near-human or animal-like monster. It appears in haze, smoke, or mist.

Technique As in the previous exercise, different ways of producing textures are shown. Though the child attaches great importance to the limiting outline, we try in this case (fourth grade) to do without it and to create these textures directly, evenly, and not too arbitrarily.

The paper can be placed upright or lengthwise. The smooth side of the paper is used.

Each child tries to draw several ghosts, giving each ghost its own texture. Sizes can vary greatly, and overlapping is permissible.

This drawing was done in the fourth grade (nine to ten years).

Similar Subjects: (The technique is particularly suitable for the depiction of movement.) ice hockey / ski slope / mirage / fire brigade / escape / harvest time / Indians / insects / chimney sweep / battle / rabbit / cat/ screech owl / trees in the wind / locomotive / marten / men from Mars / mouse / man in the moon / marmot / panther / pirates / band of robbers / smoking factory chimneys / rain / raining cats and dogs / rhythmical exercises / a flock of sheep / story of creation / swimming / sunrise / heavy gale / dance.

Brush Drawing

Direct brush drawing, whether in rhythmic and linear movements or in blots, corresponds to the quick working method of the child. It loosens, frees, and is an excellent introduction to painting. Small children draw in this way, even before they reach school age.

Here, too, there must be no preliminary drawing. It is advisable to begin with ink, drawing ink, or well-diluted watercolor, keeping at first to one color.

Effects will depend greatly on the quality of the paper, on its hardness or softness, its smoothness, or its ability to absorb. Newsprint is again highly suitable. A colored background should be used from time to time.

In the first and second grade, emphasis will be on line and rhythm, in the third and fourth on dots, patches, etc.

Hair and bristle brushes should be used; they must never be left in water.

Brush Drawing I. Ink Drawing: The Family Walk

Materials   Sable and bristle brush; ink; newsprint, about 15 inches by 12 inches.

Subject   The lesson begins with a short introductory talk, discussing the appearance of the individual members of the family, spacing, etc.

Technique   The right way of holding the brush should be explained to the children. Lines can be fine, wide, flowing, or interrupted; areas are of varying sizes, more or less clearly outlined. Textures are formed by dots, small patches, etc. In painting, the child's arm should not rest on the table but should move freely.

The paper is placed horizontally. Figures are painted direct without any preliminary drawing. The largest figure can touch the edges of the paper above and below. Figures should differ as much as possible (sweaters, hats, trousers, socks, etc.).

This drawing was done in the first grade (six to seven years).

Similar Subjects: (Everything that can be painted with a brush can also be drawn with a brush. The important thing is the contrast between light and dark.) monkey / blackbird / apple tree / artist / tree in bloom / clown / David and Goliath / duck / pheasant / fish / escape / goose / the goose girl / garden / giraffe / cock / witch / chicken / dog / Indian / insects / fun fair / chimney sweep / rabbit / cat / screech owl / king / crab / crocodile / cow / leopard / dandelion / locomotive / mask / tribal dance / Neptune / peacock / horse racing / pirate / robber / rider / reindeer / knight / Robinson Crusoe / sheep / swimming / tightrope-walker / self-portrait / soldiers / sport / Santa Claus / bull / fir tree / dance / tiger / jungle / cattle market / birds / winter day / wolf / zebra / goat / circus / zoo.

Brush Drawing II. Cattle

Materials   Same as in the previous exercise, using drawing ink instead of ordinary ink; smooth white paper, 24 inches by 10 inches; newsprint for experimenting.

Subject   Here, emphasis is on the plane rather than the line. The lesson begins with a short introductory talk in which the chief characteristics of the cow are pointed out to the children (the head is triangular in profile, V-shaped from the front, horns point upward, etc.). A sketch on the blackboard will prove helpful, particularly to city children.

Technique   Each cow should be given different markings. There should be no background, because the children's drawings are meant to be joined together afterwards. Each child should draw several cows, one behind the other. Again, there is to be no preliminary drawing. Direct brush drawing compels the child to concentrate on form and technique.

This drawing was done in the second grade (seven to eight years).

Similar subjects: ant / ant heap / blackbirds in a cherry tree / aquarium / arctic regions / car / station / ball game / bee / slowworm / blackberry / buffalo / clown / cathedral / village / dragon / kite in the air / lizard / railway / polar bear / jackdaw / factory / pheasant / at the window / fish / fishing port / flamingo / football team / the goose girl / giraffe / city / harbor / cock / harlequin / witch / a witch's house / shepherd and his flock / bride and bridegroom / bumblebee / breeds of dog / initials / jaguar / fun fair / species of beetle / cage with panther / chimney sweep / rabbit / fighting bulls / cat / leopard / bookmark / dandelion / locomotive / ladybird / machines / mask / sea gull / tribal dance / North Pole / ornament / palace / panther / parrot / peacock / horse racing / caterpillar / boa constrictor/ Robinson Crusoe / sheep / tortoise / snake / butterfly / snail shell / story of creation / swallow / pig / sunflower / bull / beach / trolley / pinewood / dance / carpet / devil / tiger / national costumes / jungle / traffic signs / cattle market / birds / forest / design for weaving / wild duck / winter / desert journey / zebra / camping ground / goat / circus / zoo.

Brush Drawing III. Diluted Poster Colors: At the Fair

Materials   Sable and bristle brushes; dark, diluted poster colors; paper of a bright, comparatively light color, 12 inches by 5 inches; newsprint for experimenting.

Subject   The lesson begins with a short introductory talk about the life of the fair—people with baskets and sacks, farmers' wives, children, old men, farmers, dogs, horses and carts. One or two people can be described, perhaps a man with a top hat, stiff collar, cravat, gloves, and cane.

Technique   Again, there should be no preliminary drawing. The figures appear as silhouettes, enlivened by buttons, boot laces, unkempt hair, kerchiefs, etc. Later, the scissor cut (see page 107) can be developed from these drawings.

This drawing was done in the fourth grade (nine to ten years).

Similar Subjects: monkey / ant / blackbird / angler / aquarium / workman / artists / doctor / old automobile / baker / at the station / bear / construction worker / broom-maker / postman / buffalo / Tom Thumb / David and Goliath / village band/ squirrel / Eskimo / bicyclist / family outing / fire brigade / heron / flamingo / escape / football player / the goose girl / vegetable woman / Puss in Boots / giraffe / a journey by gondola / cock / harlequin / peddler / witch / stag / the shepherd and his flock / wedding / woodcutter / chicken / bumblebee / dog / hedgehog / Indian / insects / the hunter / Joseph and Mary / cacti / camel / cat / the three wise men from the East / cow / teacher / leopard / sea gull / dandelion / locomotive / rabble / ladybird / painter / bricklayer / mouse / military inspection / lion / marmot / rhinoceros / Neptune / hippopotamus / orchestra / panther / horse / pirate / robber / caterpillar / deer / rider / reindeer / giant / knight / Robinson Crusoe / sheep / blacksmith / snail / Snow White and the Seven Dwarfs / educational trip / sea horse / sailboat / skier / soldiers / sport / Santa Claus / bull / stork / swimming pool / on the trolley / dance / tug of war / William Tell / devil / gymnast / moving house / cattle market / birds / population census / competition / the goblins / ram / weasel / wolf / desert journey / magician / goat / gypsy / circus / zoo / dwarf.

Charcoal and Chalk Drawing

Charcoal can be used as early as the first grade. Medium-hard or soft grades are preferable, broken into convenient lengths (about 2 inches). Charcoal can be used both for line drawing (thick rather than thin strokes) and for texture (held horizontally).

Charcoal is particularly suitable for work on a larger scale and for sketching. It helps towards a general loosening and encourages a feeling for the contrasting effects of light and darkness.

Since charcoal smudges, a fixative should be used. Charcoal is easily wiped off, and corrections therefore present no difficulty. Fairly large sheets of paper, preferably of a coarse-grained variety, are best. Black chalk (oil pastels, graphite, etc.) can be used like charcoal, though it will produce a somewhat darker effect. Only pastels require a fixative.

Large sheets for charcoal and chalk drawing are best fastened on a wall. Themes with distinctly linear or light-and-dark effects should be chosen. The technique is suitable for use throughout the primary school.

Charcoal Drawing I. Soft Charcoal: Chimney Sweep

Materials   Charcoal, for each pupil a piece measuring about 2 inches; gray paper, about 16 inches by 10 inches (possibly larger); fixative spray.

Subject   The lesson begins with a short introductory talk about the chimmey sweep (black face, white teeth, brush, etc.). Objects unknown to the children are shown on the blackboard.

Technique   The charcoal is held like blackboard chalk. Gentle pressure produces light shades, stronger pressure dark gray to black. It must be realised that charcoal is brittle and smudges easily. Thin lines can be drawn with the edge of the charcoal; whole areas can be filled in by placing its entire width on the paper. The figure should fill the height of the page.

If necessary, a preliminary faint outline also in charcoal can be drawn. All the possibilities of this material, which will be new to the children, should be tried out. Particularly good work can be preserved with fixative.

This drawing was done in the first grade (six to seven years).

Similar Subjects: monkey / blackbird / slums / artists / station / bear / broom-maker / buffalo / clown / demon / dragon / oakwood / railway / jackdaw / donkey / factory / mirage / escape / goose / ghost / spirit / harlequin / witch / dog / jaguar / camel / rabbit / cat / the coalman / coal mine / charcoal-burner / deciduous tree / leopard / lion / locomotive / marten / man from Mars / man in the moon / marmot / mask / rhinoceros / hippopotamus / panther / robber / giant / sport / bull / pigeon / carpet / devil / tiger / monster / jungle / design for weaving / wolf / magician / zebra / goat / circus / zoo.

Ruth Spori

Peter

Charcoal Drawing II. Indian Chief

Materials   Same as in the previous exercise, using wrapping paper, about 18 inches by 14 inches.

Subject   The lesson begins with a short introductory talk, pointing out the characteristics of the Indian chief: aquiline nose, feathered headdress, smooth hair, wide trousers, quiver with bow and arrows, moccasins, tomahawk, etc.

Technique   This is entirely a line drawing. The children should be shown the way to draw thin, wide, or delicates lines, etc. The hand must not touch the paper, and corrections should be kept to the absolute minimum. The paper is placed lengthwise, the figure taking up as much space as possible. It is permissible to sketch the drawing first in outline. Good examples should be preserved with fixative.

This drawing was done in the t h i r d grade (eight to nine years).

Similar Subjects: rhythmical exercises with both hands such as circles, waves, smoke, letters of the alphabet / monkey / artist / dredger / bear / broom-maker / buffalo / castle / clown / David and Goliath / cathedral / dragon / squirrel / pheasant / haul of fish / bat / garden / ghosts / Puss in Boots / cock / hamster / harlequin / peddler / witch / stag / shepherd / chicken / dog / hedgehog / the huntsmen / cage / the battle of the knights / crane / crocodile / teacher and his pupils / man from Mars / machine / mask / ocean / church / rhinoceros / hippopotamus / oasis / palm tree / lake dwelling / the Trojan Horse / pirate / pirate ship / bicycle racing / robber / rider / giant / boa constrictor / Robinson Crusoe / a flock of sheep / snake / story of creation / sunflower / Santa Claus / bull / on the trolley / heavy gale / dancer / devil / tropical island / monster / jungle / cattle market / scarecrow / forest / wharf / competition / windmill / winter / wolf / skyscraper / magician / gypsy / circus / zoo.

Charcoal Drawing III. Contrasts of Light and Dark: A Zebra

Materials   Same as in the first charcoal exercise, using light-brown wrapping paper.

Subject   The lesson begins with a short introductory talk about the main features of the zebra: rounder than horse or donkey, with shorter ears than a donkey and a short, erect mane. The stripes on head and legs run in different directions. The zebra should be shown in several actions (walk, trot, canter).

Technique   Here, the emphasis is on the plane rather than the line. The children should be shown how the stripes can be formed without first drawing outlines. Stripes follow the natural shape of the body, broadening towards the middle and narrowing on the legs.
The zebra can be sketched in outline. It should fill the entire sheet (placed lengthwise). Great care must be taken to avoid smudging. Good examples should be preserved with fixative.

This drawing was done in the fourth grade (nine to ten years).

Similar Subjects: monkey / African totem / ant / bathing suit / bee / clown / decorative works / cathedral / dragon / lizard / jackdaw / duck / pheasant / fish in nets / flamingo / frog / football team / goose / giraffe / harlequin / wedding / bumblebee / dog / Indian carpet / initials / jaguar / rabbit / cat / cow / leopard / ladybird / mask / native dance / ornameut / palace / panther / peacock / caterpillar / rider / boa constrictor / sheep / tortoise / snake / bull / pigeon / carpet / tiger / national costumes / birds / desipn for weaxing / wild duck / winter / goat / circus / zoo.

Black Wax Crayon Drawing. The Contrast of Light and Dark: White Stag

Materials   Black wax crayon (or pastel, etc.); white cartridge paper, about 14 inches by 10 inches.

Subject   The lesson begins with a short introductory talk about the main features of the stag: a proud animal with big antlers, gracefully curved neck, long thin legs (compare with horse), hooves like sheep and cows.

Technique   The paper is placed lengthwise. The stag is drawn in precise outline with the sharp edge of the crayon. The animal figure, extending over the whole page, is formed by its background, which is completely filled in, until the stag stands out in its full radiance. To avoid smudging, the hand should rest on a sheet of paper. Only pastel drawings require a fixative.

This drawing was done in the third grade (eight to nine years). Colored paper can also be used.

Similar Subjects: monkey / arctic landscape / artist / blackbird / automobile / baker / ballet dancer / flowering twig / buffalo / clown / David and Goliath / thistle / cathedral / dragon / lizard / polar bear / jackdaw / angel / owl / pheasant / firebird / fish / heron / flamingo / lilac / football player / goose / the goose girl / Puss in Boots / giraffe / cock / wedding coach / chicken / bumblebee / dog / jaguar / beetle / camel / rabbit / chestnut blossom / cat / centaur / the three wise men from the East / cook / crane / cow / leopard / lion / locomotive / Lucifer / machine / sea gull / night / daffodils / rhinoceros / hippopotamus / ornament / panther / peacock / horse / deer / rider / reindeer / Robinson Crusoe / snow / story of creation / swan / swimmer / sailboats / tightrope-walker / spider / sport / bull / stork / dance / pigeon.

B. Painting Techniques

Painting with Colored Pencils

Colored pencils are used for both painting and drawing. They are particularly suitable for detailed work on a small scale. Small children (first grade and earlier) use colored pencils for linear narrative outline drawings. Older children (second grade and later) at first fill in only outlined objects; later they cover the entire page.

A smooth paper should be used. Except for line drawings, a small format is preferable. A limited color range encourages color sense and imagination. Most colored pencil drawings suffer from a profusion of colors, careless strokes, and excessive size.

Subjects dominated by color and involving few objects should be chosen.

Painting in colored pencils is suitable throughout the primary grades.

Painting with Colored Pencils I. A Cat

Materials   Colored pencils—brown, yellow, black, blue; ordinary pencil; eraser; light-gray paper, about 5 inches by 3 inches; sandpaper for sharpening pencils.

Subject   The lesson begins with a short introductory talk about the chief characteristics of the cat: a round head with pointed ears, long, narrow body, short legs, sharp claws, long tail, etc. Cats can be of various colors. Different positions should be shown.

Technique   Here, in one of the first projects of this kind undertaken with the children, the emphasis will be on the colored line. The cat is first lightly outlined in pencil. The outline is then rubbed off, so that nothing but a faint shadow remains. It is also possible to begin with paler colors, using darker shades over them.

The paper is placed lengthwise, and the cat fills the entire sheet. Finally, the hairs of the coat are drawn with short, distinct strokes. The hairs stand up slightly towards the edge.

An alternative would be to draw a several cats on a larger sheet of paper about 16 inches by 3 inches.

This picture was painted in the first grade (six to seven years).

Similar subjects: all animals with distinct silhouettes / sunset / in the streetcar / trees / clown / prisoner / flowers / swimmer / birds / ballet dancer.

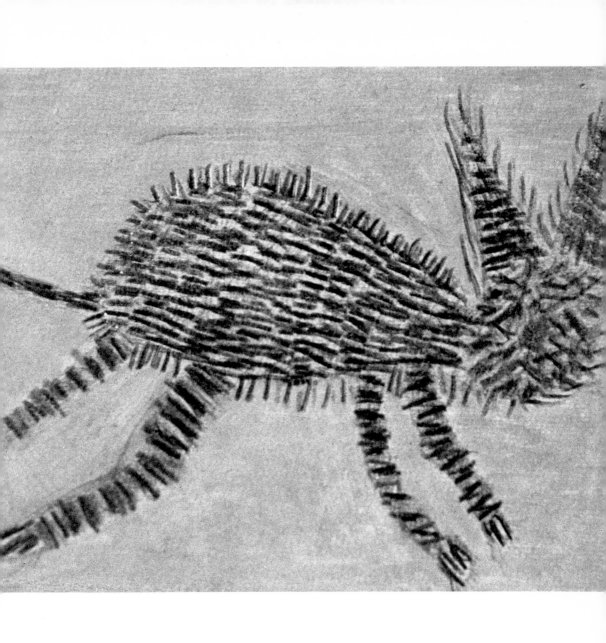

Painting with Colored Pencils II. Santa Claus

Materials   Colored pencils—red, black, white, gray, ocher; ordinary pencil; eraser; sheet of white paper, about 6 inches by 4 inches.

In this type of work, where the emphasis is on the plane rather than the line, it is particularly important to work on a small scale, since it is extremely difficult to fill in large areas with the point of a pencil.

Subject   The lesson begins with a short introductory talk about the chief characteristics of Santa Claus: a dignified old man, dressed in a red coat and hood trimmed with fur, a sack filled with presents on his back, etc. He walks through the winter landscape, accompanied by his reindeer.

Technique   The children are shown how to color whole areas. Mixed colors are applied lightly, pure colors more strongly. Shading—in the same direction throughout each area—must be done with great care. It is better to keep to a limited range of color at the beginning; this will teach the children to mix colors.

The figure is sketched in outline in pencil (to be rubbed out so that only the faintest trace remains for guidance) or colored pencil. The figure should fill the entire sheet (placed lengthwise). The effect of snowflakes is produced by letting the paper show through.

This picture was painted by children in the s e c o n d grade (seven to eight years).

Similar Subjects: evening sun / monkey / ant / blackbird / angler / artist / automobile / aster / the bed of a stream / baker / balloon woman / bear / broom-maker / bee / flowering twig / postman / blackberry / buffalo / clown / tiler / dahlia / Tom Thumb / decorative works / thistle / village / dragon / branch of an oak / squirrel / lizard / elephant / duck / strawberry / donkey / owl / fern / pheasant / spotted salamander / thimble / fish / heron / flamingo / lilac / forsythia / fruit / football player / goose / gardener / birthday cake / vegetable woman / giraffe / gladioli / goldfish / laburnum / hip / cock / crowfoot / hamster / harlequin / grasshopper / raspberry / stag / shepherd / coltsfoot / chicken / bumblebee / dog / hazelnut / hedgehog / Icarus / Indian / insects / the hunter / jaguar / red currant / jewelry / beetle / camel / rabbit / chestnut blossom / cat / screech owl / crane / crocodile / cow / pebble / crab / deciduous tree / teacher / leopard / dragon fly / lion / dandelion / locomotive / Lucifer / ladybird / corncob / mask / bricklayer / mouse / butcher / sea gull / marmot / nightingale / daffodil / rhinoceros / carnation / Neptune / hippopotamus / ornament / palace / panther / parrot / peacock / horse / mushroom / robber chief / caterpillar / deer / rider / reindeer / giant / knight / Robinson Crusoe / Little Red Ridinghood / sheep / tortoise / snake / cowslip / butterfly / snail / Snow White and the Seven Dwarfs / swallow / pig / gladiolus / self-portrait / sunflower / spider / design for embroidery / bull / pansy / stork / fir tree / pigeon / carpet / devil / animals / tiger / tomato / national costumes / gymnast / monster / violet / forget-me-not / birds / the golden bird / animals of the woods / design for weaving / plantain / Christmas tree / ram / weasel / wild duck / wolf / cloud / at the dentist / magician / zebra / news vendor / goat / gypsy / dwarf / onion.

Painting with Colored Pencils III. Exploiting all the Possibilities of this Technique: A Parrot

Materials   All available colors; lead pencil; eraser; white or light-colored paper, about 8 inches by 6 inches.

Subject   The lesson begins with a short introductory talk about the main features of a parrot: it resembles larger birds in size, but, unlike them, it is brightly colored. Its beak is curved, its eyes seem almost like buttons, and it often has a crest.

Technique   Every color can be used for the outlines. The different areas will be of pure or mixed colors. Lines should be lively and not forced. If possible, there should be no preliminary outline drawing. When a lead pencil is used first, the lines should be rubbed out to leave only a faint trace. The figure should fill the whole of the upright sheet.

This picture was painted in the t h i r d grade (eight to nine years).

Similar Subjects: apple harvest / aquarium / Noah's ark / a group of artists / traffic / on the stream / in the bakery / at the seashore / station / ball games / building site / farm / beehive / flower garden / a bunch of flowers / botanical gardens / at the well / castle / David and Goliath / village band / railway / ice hockey match / icebergs / a choir of angels / Eskimo / factory / family / mirage / at the window / holiday episode / conflagration / haul of fish / escape / airport / football match / the goose girl / birthday party / vegetable market / Puss in Boots / city in fog / harbor / house building / pedlar / autumnal wood / harvest time / a witch's house / the shepherd and his flock / wedding banquet / wedding coach / Indian family / the fox hunt / fun fair / at the jeweler / cage with animals / calendar / journey by camel / merry-go-round / in the shop / the three wise men from the East / teacher and pupils / the blue light / favorite occupation / rabbit / painter at work / market day / men from Mars / ocean bed / the military / man in the moon / night / a field of daffodils / Fairy Godmother / at the North Pole / oasis / fruit-picking / Venetian or Oriental palace / palm island / paradise / day of departure / episode on a journey / Robinson Crusoe / Little Red Ridinghood / shop window / me asleep / castle / blacksmith / snowplow / Snow White and the Seven Dwarfs / tailor / story of creation / joiner / shoemaker / educational trip / classroom / swallow / pig / swimming / trip in a sailboat / tightrope-walker / skiing / soldiers / summer / sunset / sport / town / at the seashore / swimming pool / on the trolley / room / dance / tug of war / pond / William Tell / theater / deep sea diver / at the table / national costumes / dream / tropical island / gym lesson / moving house / jungle / my greatest pleasure / auto accident / cattle / market / birds / the golden bird / population census / wood / animals in the woods / aquatic bird / Christmas / wharf / competition / the goblins / winter day / living room / journey through the desert / campsite / gypsy / carpenter / circus / zoo.

Painting with Colored Pencils IV. Carpet in Chequered Design

Materials   All available colors; lead pencil; eraser; white paper, about 10 inches by 10 inches.

Subject   Here, the subject plays a very subordinate part.

Technique   Our carpet mesures 8 inches by 8 inches. It is therefore divided into 1-inch squares which are outlined in lead pencil. Care must be taken to remove the pencil lines as far as possible before applying the colors. Each square must be a different color. When colors are mixed—*i.e.*, applied in layers—shading should always be done in the same direction. Mixed and pure colors alternate throughout.

This picture was painted in the fourth grade (nine to ten years). The illustration is on a considerably larger scale than the original to give some indication of the technical problems.

Similar Subjects: apples / beehive / flower garden / castle wall / design for a kite / invitation cards / flag / haul of fish / bird's-eye view of a garden / vegetable stall / decorative motif for a bookcover / gates of heaven / wigwam / initials / calendar / bookmark / fruit basket / fruit dish / ornament / designs for ornament / front of a palace / parrot / snake / butterfly wing / snail shell / bird's-eye view of a schoolyard / design for embroidery / pansy / timetable / carpet (geometrical forms) / motifs for plants and animals / place cards / national costumes / jungle / wood.

Painting with Colored Chalks

Oil and wax crayons, pastels, and blackboard chalks allow much freer effects than ordinary colored pencils. Though they can be used for outline drawings, they are much more suitable for work over whole areas. Oil and wax crayons can produce a vast range of mixed colors. Like blackboard chalks, they also lend themselves to sgraffito, a scraping technique impossible with colored pencils.

Pastels smudge very easily and must therefore be treated with fixative.

Though almost any kind of paper can be used, finely grained or smooth paper of a fairly large size will be found preferable. Rougher paper is more suitable for pastels.

Subjects demanding the use of bright colors should be chosen. Work with colored chalks should continue throughout the primary school.

Painting and drawing on the blackboard, or on large sheets of paper, should be practised extensively. Throughout drawing lessons, the children ought to have the blackboard available for practice.

The advantage of this technique lies in the facility with which work can be corrected, the large size, and the freedom it allows. Work on coarse-textured paper is treated with fixative. The children's own work on the blackboard also forms a lively and stimulating form of decoration for the classroom.

Painting with Colored Chalks I. Oil Crayons: Self-Portrait

Materials   Oil crayons; white paper, about 14 inches by 10 inches.

Subject   The lesson begins with a short introductory talk about different physical types. Everybody is encouraged to discover his own principal features. The head might be narrow or wide, with a low or high hairline. Attention is also drawn to the color of hair and eyes, size and shape of the mouth, body build, dress, etc.

Technique   Oil and wax crayons are held as close to the tip as possible. The emphasis can be on line or on area; in the second case lighter colors should be mixed with white to increase their radiance. Colors are applied either by shading or by circular movements. In mixing, the lighter colors should be applied over the darker. A certain amount of experiment will be found inevitable. The ground of the paper will gradually disappear. Each new color should be applied in a different direction.

Experiments should be made with broken colors. White will be used over pure colors; gray, brown, and black underneath pure colors.

Mistakes can be corrected by scraping off the color with a sharp knife. If necessary, lines can be drawn first in pencil (to be rubbed off again) or in a paler color.

The paper is held vertically. The head or figure should cover the entire sheet.

The aim of this exercise is to exploit the possibilities of the technique to the utmost.

The examples shown are the work of children in the first grade (right) and the third grade (left). The younger child still draws himself full length; he cannot think of the head in isolation, while the portrait presents no difficulty to the child in the third grade.

Similar Subjects: evening sun / monkey / apple tree / aquarium / Noah's ark (animals) / station / farm / bunch of flowers / flowering tree / botanical gardens / clown / dahlias / village / Sleeping Beauty / dragon / railway / elephant ride / donkey / pheasant / fish / fishing port / lilac / frog / football player / fox / goose / cock / harlequin / building houses / autumnal tree / wedding / woodcutter / chicken / dog / beetle / calendar / crocodile / cow / leopard / dandelion / locomotive / ocean bed / Negro / Neptune / oasis / fruit harvest / palace / palms / parrot / lake dwelling / peacock / horse / robber / rider / giant / knight / Robinson Crusoe / story of creation / educational trip / summer / sun / sunflower / sport / Santa Claus / village dance / jungle wood / Christmas / desert / magic gardens / goat / circus / zoo / dwarf.

Painting with Colored Chalks IV. Exercise with Pastels or Blackboard Chalks on a Dark Background (Blackboard)

Materials   Colored pencil (light color); one or several pieces of blackboard chalk (light color) per pupil; eraser; blackboards or black paper, about 16 inches by 16 inches; fixative spray.

Technique   We first draw zigzag lines across the entire field in colored pencil, moving from the upper left to the lower right. These lines can be quite irregular, although they should not be too close. The forms are then filled like a chessboard (alternate squares), beginning at the upper left edge and taking care to avoid smudging.

Several light shades of chalk can be used. The finished work is preserved with fixative.

This painting was done in the s e c o n d grade (seven to eight years). The subject is equally suitable for oil colors.

Similar Subjects: apples / bed of a stream / beehive / slowworm / invented flowers / castle wall / dahlia / dragon / the skin of a lizard (magnified) / invitation cards / fish (scales) / fruit dish / fruit basket / bird's-eye view of a garden / birthday cake / vegetable stall / harlequin / witch's house / initial / calendar / pebbles / bookmark / the leaves of dandelion / corncob / a field of daffodils / ornament / design for ornaments / front of palace / boa constrictor / tortoise / snake / snail shell / field of sunflowers / carpet / place cards / magic gardens / chessboard.

Painting with Colored Chalks V. Designing Patterns

Materials   Oil crayons; white or gray paper, about 14 inches by 10 inches; lead pencil; eraser; ruler.

Subject   The task is to design simple patterns which can later be used in decoration.

According to age groups, we evolve several patterns from the simplest motifs (see page 14). It is important here to impress on the children the nature of ornament, the motif, its arrangement, and its repetition. The children proceed as they would in dictation.

Technique   First Year:

a) The whole sheet is filled in, using the smooth side. A simple zigzag line is drawn in black over a width of about 1¹/₂ inches.

b) The pattern is repeated, except that a second zigzag line, which bisects the first, is now introduced. The diamonds formed by these two lines are filled in with alternating colors.

c) The diamond pattern is repeated, as in b, but using different—again alternating—colors, only filling half of each diamond.

a, b, and a are then repeated.

Second Year:

The sheet of paper, about 12 inches by 6 inches, placed horizontally and using the smooth side, is divided into three squares of equal size. The children are then shown how to draw three smaller squares inside each large square. Distances between the squares should not be regular. The first group of four squares are then filled in, using no more than three colors (a). Mixed colors only are employed; the first and third squares should have the same color. The colors are reversed in the next group of squares (b). The last group (c) is merely a repetition of a.

Third Year:

The paper, in this case light gray, is placed horizontally. The smooth side is used. A thin line is then drawn in pencil about 1 inch from the upper and lower edges.

a) The motif (about 1 to 1¹/₂ inches high) is repeated in pencil along this line.

b) It is then repeated below at a smaller distance (x).

c) The fields are filled in with two or three mixed colors.

Here, we have different possibilities (c, d, e).

Strong emphasis should be placed on the contrast between light and dark. Colors should be mixed and applied with great care.

Fourth Year:

Colored paper is used about 10 inches by 10 inches, working on the smooth side. The children should be shown how to proceed on the blackboard.

a) A line is drawn with the ruler 1 inch from the edge.

b) The square thus formed is divided twice across its height and twice across its width.

c) Diagonals are then drawn, and the resultant areas are filled with pure or mixed colors, using one pair of colors in each row, and taking care not to have the same color in adjoining areas. Two different colors are used in the second row. The third row follows the pattern of the first, the fourth that of the second. Great emphasis should be placed on contrasting effects.

Similar Subjects: dragon / birthday cake / initials / Indian / necklace / calendar / bookmark / the cloak of a king / mask / ornament / design for ornaments / front of palace / boa constrictor / tortoise / snake / butterfly / jewelry / snail shell / carpet / place cards / national costumes.

I

II

a   b   c (a)

III

a

b   x

d   e

d   e   f

IV

g   h

c   c   c

Painting with Colored Chalks VI. Oil Crayon on Colored Ground: A Snail

Materials   Oil crayons; dark-blue paper, about 10 inches by 14 inches.

Subject   The lesson begins with a short introductory talk about the principal features of the snail: head with two pairs of horns, a larger pair above and a smaller pair below; a long body which supports the shell, whose spiral fields are decorated in simple linear designs (see page 14). Blades of grass form a lively background.

Technique   The paper is placed lengthwise and the smooth side used. The figure of the snail fills the entire page. Choice of color should be left to the children. Light colors will show up best.

These pictures were done in the t h i r d grade (eight to nine years).

Similar Subjects: evening sun / switchback / monkey / blackbird / apple tree / aquarium / Noah's ark / arctic regions / artists / a long line of cars / bakery / at the seashore / station / ballet / ball games / building site / farm / beehive / flower garden / flower basket / wreath of flowers / bunch of flowers / flowering tree / botanical gardens / buffalo / castle / clown / dahlia / Tom Thumb / David and Goliath / Sleeping Beauty / dragon / oakwood / squirrel / lizard / railway / angel / duck / Eskimo / factory / family / at the window / holiday / fish / fishing port / heron / flamingo / escape / frog / fruit / football / the goose girl / garden / gardener / vegetable woman / Puss in Boots / giraffe / gladioli / goldfish / city / harbor / cock / harlequin / autumnal fruit / witch / stag / shepherd and his flock / wedding coach / woodcutter / chicken house / dog / Indian / insects / the hunt / jaguar / beetle / cage / rabbit / merry-go-round / chestnut blossom / cat / screech owl / crane / deciduous tree / teacher / leopard / lighthouse / favorite occupation / lion / dandelion / goose / Lucifer / ladybird / painter / market day / mask / mouse / ocean bed / the military / sea gull / oasis / fruit-picking / ornament / palace / desert island / parrot / paradise / peacock / mushrooms / pirate / prince and princess / robber / rainy weather / journey / rider on horseback / giant / boa constrictor / knight / Robinson Crusoe / Little Red Ridinghood / a flock of sheep / shop window / ship / tortoise / sleep / snake / butterfly / snow / Snow White and the Seven Dwarfs / story of creation / educational trip / swimming / sailboat / tight-rope-walker / self-portrait / skier / soldiers / summer / sunflower / spider / sportsman / Santa Claus / town / starry night / design for embroidery / bull / pansy / stork / on the beach / swimming pool / on the trolley / room / pinewood / dance / pigeon / pond / carpet / William Tell / devil / theater / deep sea diver / tiger / national costumes / dream / tropical island / moving house / jungle / cattle market / birds / scarecrow / competition / winter / desert / magic gardens / zebra / campsite / goat / circus / zoo / dwarf.

Painting with Colored Chalks VII. Line Drawing with Blackboard Chalks or Pastels: A Cathedral

Materials   Pastels or blackboard chalks; thick black paper, about 18 inches by 24 inches (or blackboards); fixative; fixative spray.

Subject   The lesson begins with a brief introductory talk. Only the principal façade of the cathedral is drawn. The lowest portion resembles a house, with a center door and two other doors, one on each side. Above the main door is a rose window; above the others are the characteristic windows with pointed arches. Some churches have only one tower, others may have a spire, a dome, etc. Drawings or photographs of churches can be shown.

Technique   Only light colors are used. Emphasis throughout is on the effect of the line. The church fills the entire (upright) sheet. The different portions of the façade are filled in with linear ornament. The hand must never be allowed to touch the paper if smudging is to be avoided. Finished work is preserved with fixative.

These drawings were done in the fourth grade (nine to ten years). Oil crayons can be used similarly.

Similar Subjects: Noah's ark / the bed of a stream / dredger / railroad station / bee / botanical gardens / fortress / roofs of the city / dahlia / thistle / dragon / oakwood / train / a choir of angels / factory / bicycle / fern / thimble / fish / fishing port / airplane / galley / garden / procession of ghosts / giraffe / city / harbour / cock / building a house / plan of a house / grasshopper / a witch's house / gates of heaven / skyscraper / chicken house / dog racing / hedgehog / Indian / crown of jewels / cage with animals / cacti / merry-go-round / chervil / church porch / crane / crocodile / dragonfly / dandelion / corncob / machine / mask / musical instruments / native huts / oasis / orchestra / palace / gates of heaven / lake dwellings / Trojan Horse / pirate ship / cycle racing / caterpillar / under the umbrella / bowling a hoop / boa constrictor / Robinson Crusoe / a flock of sheep / shipbuilding / snake / castle / jewelry / snail shell / snowflake / sea horse / tightrope-walker / ski lift / sunflower / spider / town / walking on stilts / stars / design for embroidery / trolley / time-table / dance / carpet / place cards / jungle thicket / wharf / tools / Viking ship / ram / windmill / skyscraper / magic gardens / robot / dream house / tent / goat / circus / zoo.

Painting with Poster Colors

Painting with poster colors should begin in the first grade. This technique offers a range of infinite possibilities: outline painting, brush drawing, and filling in the contours (line and plane); painting with and without preliminary drawing (pencil, charcoal); painting with colored washes (watercolor); painting with opaque colors (tempera); mixing techniques (gouache); painting with a limited range of colors; wet-in-wet painting, etc. All these techniques serve, above all, to develop the sense of color (see page 13). In no other medium are colors mixed as easily as here; the child literally discovers new colors. The choice of color becomes an immediate problem, and the child's effort to come to terms with color are therefore intensified. Painting with poster colors should be encouraged accordingly, though not at the expense of humbler techniques that may produce less startling results.

Almost any kind of paper can be used, although absorbent varieties will be found preferable. Dimensions should be no less than 12 inches by 8 inches. The different media and techniques are described below.

Tempera	Opaque medium. The color is put on thickly; the ground is completely covered. This medium is particularly suitable for younger children. Colors are mixed on the palette with only a little water.
Watercolor (colored washes)	Transparent medium. The colors are mixed with plenty of water, so that the paper is allowed to shine through. Here, "mixing colors" means applying one wash over another. This method of painting requires technical experience and maturity. It is therefore unsuitable for the primary grades, though this does not mean its effects cannot be produced by younger children; it simply is not taught.
Gouache	Opaque (tempera) and transparent (watercolor) painting combined.
Wet-in-wet painting	This technique can be tried occasionally. Clean water is drawn over the paper with a sponge. Wetting the back of the paper will smooth it out. We can now draw powerful lines, shapes or structures on the still wet ground. The colors will dissolve more or less. If the paper is too wet, the forms disintegrate. It can always be dampened again. The paper sticks to the table because of the water, without any drawing pins, etc.
Colored washes	Pencil, charcoal, and particularly pen and ink drawings can be enlivened with transparent colored washes.

Poster Colors I. Introduction to Painting with Poster Colors: Cat

Materials Poster colors; black and red water jar; sponge; mixing bowls; bristle and sable brushes; bright-yellow paper, about 16 inches by 12 inches.

Subject The lesson begins with a brief introductory talk. A spitting tomcat with an arched back is frightening the robbers. The yellow background and the red and black of the animal are meant to express the ghostlike and the monstrous. The cat has slanting, gleaming eyes (slits of the ground color could be used for these), its hairs bristle with anger (back, legs, tail). See the cat on page 53.

Technique If a table is used instead of drawing boards, it should be covered with newspapers. It is advisable to limit the color range for the first exercise, and to mix the colors—in this case red and black—in little bowls. The children are shown how to hold the brush, how to dip it into the paint, and how to get rid of superfluous color on the edge of the bowl. Neither hand nor arm should rest on the table. Too much paint on the brush produces blots; too little will show brushmarks. With every change of color, the brush has to be cleaned in water and wiped with the sponge. The paint is put on in lines (contour as well as structural lines), over areas, and as texture (dots, dashes, dabs, circles, etc.). Colors can be painted over if they are allowed to dry first. Every painting exercise should be tried on scrap paper first. The format will be horizontal. The cat should be as big as possible. We start with a brush drawing. Normally only one color is chosen for this purpose, although several could be used (see page 38). Leftover color can be used up to paint scrap paper for collages.

The example shown was done in the first grade (six to seven years).

Similar Subjects: evening sun / monkey / blackbird / Noah's ark / animals / artist / automobile / baker / bear / mountain / flowers / flowering tree / postman / buffalo / clown / Tom Thumb / dragon / lizard / railway / ice hockey player / polar bear / duck / donkey / Eskimo / owl / pheasant / firebird / fish / frog / football player / goose / gardener / Puss in Boots / giraffe / goldfish / cock / harlequin / hare / autumnal tree / witch / stag / shepherd / chicken / bumblebee / dog / Indian / island / the hunter / jaguar / beetle / camel / rabbit / screech owl / crane / crocodile / cow / tree / leopard / lion / dandelion / locomotive / ladybird / mask / sea gull / nightingale / rhinoceros / hippopotamus / palace / palm / parrot / bird of paradise / peacock / horse / pirate / robber / deer / story of creation / self-portrait / summer / sun / sunflower / Santa Claus / stars / bull / pansy / stork / fir tree / pigeon / carpet / animals / at the table / tiger / gymnast / monster / birds / wood / Christmas tree / the goblins / wild duck / winter / wolf / magic gardens / goat / gypsy / circus people / zoo / dwarf.

Poster Colors II. Differentiation of Color: A Castle

Materials Poster colors, black, white, all yellows, brown, red; bristle brush; sponge; water jar; palette; beige paper, about 17 inches by 10 inches.

Subject The lesson begins with a brief introductory talk, pointing out the main features. The castle is situated on a hill. It consists of walls (stonework), pinnacles, loopholes, turrets (barrier), a gateway, balconies, cornices, parapets, alcoves, etc.

Technique The technique is the same as in the first exercise, except that this time the colors are mixed on the palette.

Demonstrate how to mix the colors. Place the colors in small daubs on the edge of the palette. With a brush take a bit of one color and place it in the center of the palette. Take a little water on the brush and mix it into the color. Select a second color and mix it with the first and you will get a new color. This technique is different from the technique of mixing wet colors directly on the paper.

Painting with a limited range of colors encourages the children to discover new colors by mixing and experimenting.

The format will be vertical; the castle towers into the sky. We paint directly without preliminary sketching, just roughing in a broad outline. Detail is put in afterwards.

The advantage of poster colors is that light and dark colors can be painted over each other.

This example shown was done in the first grade (six to seven years).

Similar Subjects: switchback / monkey hill / Africa / blackbird in a bush / apple-picking / Noah's ark / arctic icebreaker / slums / performing group / bed of a stream / at the seashore / station / balloon woman / building site / farm / mountain landscape / flower garden / bunch of flowers / flowering tree / botanical gardens / dahlias / cathedral / village / Sleeping Beauty / railway / ice skating / elephant / a choir of angels / Eskimo / owl / factory / family / carnival / view from the window / holiday journey / haul of fish / fishing port / lilac / the goose girl / garden / birthday / city / harbor / building houses / autumn / harvest time / a witch's house / gates of heaven / shepherds in the fields / skyscraper / wedding feast / chicken house / Indian family / the hunt / fun fair / Joseph and Mary / Joseph and his brethren / cage / camel ride / canoeist / merry-go-round / tree / teacher and pupils / favorite occupation / dandelion / locomotive / rabble / painter / market / man from Mars / machine / ocean bed / butcher / the military / man in the moon / night / field of daffodils / native village / Neptune / at the North Pole / oasis / fruit-picking / palace / paradise / lake dwellings / horse-drawn sleigh / pirate ship / rainy weather / holiday episode / knight / Robinson Crusoe / Little Red Riding-hood / a flock of sheep / in front of the shop window / sleep / Snow White and the Seven Dwarfs / story of creation / educational trip / swimming / sailboats / tightrope-walker / self-portrait / skier / soldiers / summer sunrise / town / on the beach / on the trolley / room / pond / William Tell / dream / tropical island / jungle / cattle market / scarecrow / wood / Christmas / the goblins / winter day / desert journey / magic gardens / camping holiday / circus / zoo.

Poster Colors III. The Contrast of Light and Dark: A Tree

Every color has value and hue. We distinguish within one color different degrees of lightness (value). If we arrange the value variations in their order, we will obtain the value scale of that particular color. There are also colors which are light (yellow, white) or dark (black, blue) by nature.

Every color can be lightened by gradations, using white, and darkened by gradations, using black (value scale). By juxtaposing these different values we achieve contrast between light and dark. This exercise is based on the exploitation of the contrast between light and dark.

Materials Poster colors, black, white, all greens and browns; sponge; water jar; bristle and sable brush; palette; colored paper, about 18 inches by 12 inches.

Subject We first describe the subject. The tree has a thick trunk, curving branches tapering towards the ends, out of which grow smaller branches and twigs. Part of the branch structure will be obscured by foliage: single leaves, clusters of leaves, and clumps of leaves. This will give the tree its shape.

Technique The technique shown in the first and second exercise is used with greater freedom. The values of the colors are to be changed. Mixed with white, they will become lighter tints; mixed with black, they will become darker shades. This also reduces the purity of the colors.

In our picture the clumps of leaves and the single leaves are distinguished not so much by color as by value. Every new color has its own value. Light can be painted on dark, and vice versa. Aim at the most subtle range of values. Contrasts are formed between the light tints and the dark shades.

There will be no preliminary sketch. The paper is placed upright; the tree fills the entire sheet.

The example shown was done in the s e c o n d grade (seven to eight years).

Similar Subjects: one color shaded from dark to light / another color shaded from light to dark / dividing up a given space by contrasting light and dark patches of color / a light patch among many dark colors / switchback / aquarium / arctic regions / at the doctor / stream / building site / mountain landscape in winter / flower garden / flowering twig / flowering tree / blackberry / clown / demon / David and Goliath / decorative works / cathedral / dragon / lizard / ice hockey / iceberg / angel / Eskimo / factory plant / pheasant / fire brigade / fishing port / heron / flamingo / lilac / frost / goose / the goose girl / city in winter / harbor / harlequin / a witch's house / wedding / dog / Indian / Joseph and Mary in flight / chimney sweep / rabbit / merry-go-round / chestnut blossom / shop / cook / coalman / leopard / lighthouse / dandelion / locomotive / painter / machine / butcher / sea gull / moon / daffodil / ornament / palace / panther / paradise / at the photographer's / prince / princess / Robinson Crusoe / a flock of sheep / ship / snow / story of creation / swallow / swan / sailboat / skiing / spider / town / star / design for embroidery / stork / pigeon / carpet / at the table / tiger / dream / gymnast / scarecrow / wash day / Christmas tree / weasel / winter / cloud / miracle / at the dentist / zebra / news vendor / tent / goat / circus / dwarf.

Painting with Colored Chalks II. Sgraffito—Oil Crayons: A Witch

Materials   Oil crayons; knife; nail; knitting needle or pen; sheet of paper, about 14 inches by 10 inches; lead pencil; eraser.

Subject   The lesson begins with a short introductory talk about the appearance of the witch. She is a wizened old woman, with hooked nose and pointed chin, wicked eyes, bony hands, a kerchief around her head. She carries a lantern and a bunch of keys in her hands and is followed by a cat, a raven, and an owl.

Technique   The purpose of this exercise is to demonstrate the scraping technique. At least two layers of different colors are used. Areas, lines, etc., are then scratched out of the top layer, allowing the color beneath to show through. This technique is called sgraffito (Italian: *sgraffiare*, to scratch). A knife, nail, pen, or knitting needle can be used. Mistakes are easily covered again. The paper is placed upright, using the smooth side. The figure should fill the entire sheet.
If necessary, the outline can be sketched in pencil (to be rubbed off again) or in pale oil color. Each separate form (kerchief, hair, face, eyes, lips, nose, etc.) should have a different color. The children might be limited to three colors, in which case all the others would have to be made by mixing.

This picture was painted in the s e c o n d grade (seven to eight years).

Similar Subjects: evening sun / monkey / ant / blackbird / aquarium / asters / bear / buffalo / demon / decorative works (make linear patterns) / dragon / squirrel / angel / Eskimo / owl / fern / pheasant / conflagration / fish / bat / goose girl / vegetable woman / spirit / ghost / Puss in Boots / cock / hamster / harvest time / stag / shepherd with sheep and goats / chicken / dog / hedgehog / Icarus / Red Indian / initial / jaguar / cacti / rabbit / cat / screech owl / pebbles / cow / leopard / lion / Lucifer / corncob / witch's cloak / marten / machine / mask / mouse / ocean bed / sea gull / minster / marmot / nightingale / native hut / carnation / oasis / ornament / lake dwellings / pirate / robber / caterpillar / reindeer / boa constrictor / Robinson Crusoe / flock of sheep / tortoise / snake / butterfly / snail shell / story of creation / sea horse / sunflower / cobweb with spider / town / starry night / design for embroidery / bull / fir tree / richly patterned carpet / place cards / tiger / national costumes / tropical island / flood / monster / jungle / cattle market / birds (feathers) / middle of a wood / aquatic birds / plantain / Christmas tree / ram / winter / first snow / wolf / cloud / magic gardens / zebra / goat / circus / zoo / dwarf.

Painting with Colored Chalks III. Pastels and Blackboard Chalks: A Gnome

Materials   Pastels or blackboard chalks; black coarse-grained paper, about 20 inches by 12 inches; fixative spray.

Subject   The lesson begins with a short introductory talk about the characteristics of the gnome: large head, snub nose, long beard, small body, large hands and feet, tasseled hat, pickax, shovel, sack, and lantern.

Technique   A dark background requires light colors. These can be applied as lines, over areas, or to form a texture. Dark colors will appear dull. Unlike oil crayons, pastels and blackboard chalks mix badly. Care must be taken to avoid smudging in the course of the work.
The gnome is lightly outlined in chalk; he should fill the entire (vertical) sheet. The completed drawing is preserved with fixative.

This picture was painted in the first grade (six to seven years). It is equally suitable for the blackboard or for oil colors.

Similar Subjects: monkey / ant / apple tree / aquarium / artist / doctor / baker / bear / broom-maker / bee / bunch of flowers / botanical gardens / buffalo / clown / dahlia / David and Goliath / dragon / lizard / icebergs / polar bear / jackdaw / Eskimo / owl / fish / heron / flamingo / lilac / frog / football / pheasant / goose / the goose girl / garden / Puss in Boots / cock / harlequin / building houses / pedlar / witch / a witch's house / stag / bride and bridegroom / chicken / bumblebee / dog / Indian / initial / the hunter / beetle / calendar / camel / rabbit / chestnut blossom / cat / screech owl / centaur / cook / crane / crab / crocodile / cow / leopard / dragonfly / lion / dandelion / locomotive / rabble / painter / man from Mars / mask / sea gull / man in the moon / church / daffodil / Negro / ornament / panther / parrot / peacock / pirate / princess / boa constrictor / Robinson Crusoe / sheep / tortoise / snake / butterfly / blacksmith / snail shell / snow / swallow / swan / gladiolus / sea horse / various types of sailboats / tightrope-walker / sunflower / spider / Santa Claus / starry night / bull / pansy / stork / dance / pigeon / carpet / deep sea diver / tiger / national costumes / dream / gymnast / monster / birds / washing day / aquatic birds / Christmas tree / the goblins / ram / weasel / wild duck / winter landscape / clouds / at the dentist / zebra / news vendor / goat / circus / zoo.

Poster Colors IV. Brush Drawing with Several Poster Colors: A Bicycle Race

Materials   Poster colors, black, white, ocher, scarlet, and all blues; sponge; water jar; mixing bowls; sable brush; light beige paper, about 18 inches by 8 inches.

Subject   We first explain the subject. The bicycle is a triangular shape; it has fine spoked wheels, pedals, curved handle bars with water carriers. The cyclist on a racing bicycle does not sit upright but bends forward so that his back is almost in a horizontal position. His outfit consists of a brightly striped jersey, shorts, starting number, and beret.

Technique   (See page 38.) The technique is a repetition of the different linear brush strokes (fine, broad, flowing, or interrupted).

The paper is placed lengthwise. Several cyclists are drawn as large as possible. This subject should be treated in a clear and realistic manner. As many colors as possible are mixed in the bowls. The drawings should be pinned up for criticism.

The example shown was done in the s e c o n d grade (seven to eight years). It is, however, suitable for drawing from observation in the fourth grade.

Similar Subjects: switchback / monkeys / Noah's ark / bunch of asters / bed of a stream / dredger / station / building site / beehive / bunch of flowers / botanical gardens / dahlia / cathedral / dragon / railway / ice hockey / football team / galley / garden / fern / thimble / fishing port / airplane / airport / cycling acrobats / city / harbor / cock / grasshopper / a witch's house / building a house / chicken / dog / hedgehog / Indian / insects / necklace / cage / the battle of the knights / chervil / church porch / coal mine / crane / crocodile / dragonfly / dandelion / daffodil / native huts / oasis / orchestra / ornament / palace / paradise tree / lake dwellings / the Trojan Horse / pirate ship / dollhouse / robber / caterpillar / rainy weather / rolling a hoop / rhythmical exercises / knight / Robinson Crusoe / flock of sheep / shop window / ship / a snake coiled up / the jewelry of the Queen / snail shell / sea horse / tightrope-walker / ski lift / spider / sport / town / walking on stilts / star / design for embroidery / trolley / pinewood / carpet / tiger / tropical island / gym lesson / jungle / traffic / population census / Christmas tree / tools / Viking ship / windmill / skyscraper / magic gardens / robot / dream house / tent / circus.

Poster Colors V. The Contrast of Cold and Warm Colors: Summer and Winter

Each color produces a different response. Red, yellow, and brown have a warm quality, while blue and turquoise seem completely cold. Orange is the warmest color and turquoise the coldest. To demonstrate these contrasts is the aim of this exercise. Summer colors are all yellows, reds, browns, greens, and whites; winter colors are all blues, greens, black, and white.

Materials   Sponge; palette; water jar; bristle and sable brush; sheet of paper, about 14 inches by 10 inches.

Subject   The children should give their own interpretation of a typical summer and winter subject. A few examples might be useful: hay harvest, cornfields, picking apples, summer morning, a summer's day; snow, ice, fog, skiing, tobogganing, skating, felling trees, Santa Claus, a winter's day, etc.

Technique   All the warm colors are mixed for the summer theme, exhausting every possibility. Only cold colors are mixed for the winter subject.

The children need not be told about the contrast of cold and warm colors. The subject matter and the restricted color range determine the character of the work.

Painting is done directly, without any preliminary sketching. The format can be upright or horizontal, according to the motif.

The examples shown were done in the s e c o n d grade (seven to eight years).

Similar Subjects: cold or warm effects by using various colors such as red and blue, green and blue, or red, yellow, and brown / evening sun / Africa / aquarium / arctic regions / stream / bakery / bath / blue mountains / postman / well / a fire-spitting dragon / iceberg / Eskimo / mirage / fish / frost / fire / fox / a procession of ghosts / goldfish / golden pheasant / autumnal tree / autumnal wood / gates of heaven / Icarus flying over the sea / initials / desert island / calendar / camel ride / dead leaves / lighthouse / corncob / ocean / ocean bed / North Pole / fruit / ornament / parrot / bird of paradise / peacock / mail truck / rainy day / Robinson Crusoe's shipwreck / toboggan / snow / swimming / summer / sun / sunrise / sunset / the deep sea / tropical island / whale / water / winter / winter night / winter day / winter landscape / desert / desert journey.

Poster Colors VI. The Contrast of Complementary Colors: A Mask

Any two colors which are opposites in the color circle are called complementary colors. These colors form a contrast, while at the same time complementing each other; they include red and green, orange and blue, yellow and mauve. They are deliberately used for their contrasting effect.

Materials   Poster colors, white, all reds, and greens; sable brush; sponge; water jar; palette; gray paper, about 14 inches by 10 inches.

Subject   The children are shown some masks. It is explained that the monstrous is here expressed in exaggerated forms and gaudy colors, pointing out features such as popping eyes, unkempt hair, big nose and ears, large teeth, protruding tongue and thick lips, furrows and lines.

Technique   The problem is to prompt the children into using contrast without explaining the color circle to them.
We show how to mix reds with each other and with white, contrasting the result with mixtures of greens and white. Lines, areas, and textures made up of these colors are used side by side on the mask. The paper is placed upright; the mask fills the whole sheet. We paint without a preliminary sketch.

The example shown was done in the fourth grade (nine to ten years).

Similar Subjects: Dividing up a given space by using complementary colors: blue-orange, purple-yellow, red-green.

Red-Green: apple / apple tree / apple harvest / flower / flower garden / dahlia / the palace of Sleeping Beauty / fruit / football player / a gardener in a green apron against red flowers / garden / gladioli / raspberry initials / red currant / carnation / fruit-picking / parrot / boa constrictor / Little Red Ridinghood / chessboard / snake / carpet / tomato / magic gardens / circus.

Purple-Yellow: beehive / flowers / dahlia / ice hockey team in yellow and purple colors / lilac / forsythia / fruit / gladioli / autumnal wood against purple sky / initials / leopard / lighthouse / corncob / a witch's cloak / moon / ornament / parrot / boa constrictor / chessboard / snake / butterfly / summer / sun / sunflower / starry night / pansy / carpet / violet / winter / magic gardens / circus.

Blue-Orange: bath / flowers / postman / spotted salamander / football player / goldfish / initials / jaguar / lighthouse / a magician's cloak / moon / ornament / parrot / peacock / boa constrictor / chessboard / snake / butterfly / summer / sun / carpet / tiger / desert / magic gardens / circus.

Poster Colors VII. The Contrast of Quality or Value: The Three Kings

When a pure color is mixed with white, gray, or black, it is broken. If these broken tones of one color are used next to each other, the result is a contrast of quality or value.

Materials Poster colors, black, white, all yellows and browns; bristle and sable brushes; sponge; water jar; palette; sheet of blue paper, about 20 inches by 10 inches.

Subject The lesson starts with a short introductory talk pointing out some details of the subject. The camel has two humps, big eyes, large lower lip, and large, flexible hooves; its neck stretches upward. The rider sits on or between the humps. The animals are decorated with precious carpets and bridles. The Kings have crowns, scepters, and precious gowns, carry presents, and follow the Star.

Technique The restricted color scheme obliges us to mix lighter tints of the yellows and browns by adding white and to tone them down in various degrees with gray and black.
We paint mainly two-dimensionally. The colors are applied in patches over and next to each other.
The paper is placed lengthwise. A lightly drawn preliminary pencil sketch of three large camels in a row or behind each other should be made, leaving room for the riders on top. The different quality of the color tones will show the camels up against each other.

The example shown was made in the t h i r d grade (eight to nine years).

Similar Subjects: dividing up of a given space with various shades of one or two colors / evening sun / blackbird / apple tree / aquarium / rescue operations in the arctic / slums / asters / the sales / stream / bed of a stream / at the seashore / station / flower garden / botanical gardens / herd of buffalo / chameleon / village / the palace of Sleeping Beauty / lizard / railway / elephant / donkey / owl / factory / pheasant / fish / fishing port / flamingo / lilac / frog / the goose girl / garden / vegetable stalls / ghosts / city / harbor / harlequin / hazel twig / autumnal wood / harvest time / a witch's house / gates of heaven / shepherds in the fields / chicken / dog / Indian family / insects / the hunt / fun fair / cacti in desert / chimney sweep / rabbit / cat / in the shop / pebbles / teacher and his pupils / tree / leopard / lion / dandelion / locomotive / painter / market day / bricklayer / ocean bed / butcher / military inspection / man in the moon / native huts / the North Pole / oasis / fruit / parrot / lake dwellings / an old horse / at the photographer's / smoking factory chimneys / rainy day / day of departure / reindeer / giant / boa constrictor / knight / Robinson Crusoe / a flock of sheep / snow / sheep / story of creation / shoemaker / swimming / soldiers / summer / sunflower / town / trolley / in the street / pinewood / carpet / the deep sea / tropical island / flood / jungle / cattle market / birds / bird's nest / scarecrow / population census / forest / the goblins / meadow / winter / clouds / desert / magic gardens / news vendor / herd of goats / circus / zoo / dwarf.

Poster Colors VIII. The Contrast of Intensity: A Tiger

Colors possess various degrees of intensity. Yellow is more intense than red and green, which in turn are more intense than blue. Three parts yellow, six parts red, and nine parts blue will form a balanced color scheme (see theoretical exercise). The balance between intense and less intense colors is the condition for the color harmony of a painting.

Materials   Poster colors, bright yellow and red; sponge; water jar; palette; bristle and sable brushes; sheet of bright blue paper, about 14 inches by 10 inches.

Subject   We start with a theoretical exercise (see example). The balance of intensity will form a color harmony. No theoretical explanations are given.

The characteristic features of the tiger, such as straight front legs, bent hind legs, paws, supple stretched-out body, head in profile with pronounced lower lip, and markings (stripes following the shape of the body), are pointed out to the children. The creeping tiger moves like the domestic cat.

Technique   We paint in small- and medium-sized colored dots. The paint must be applied thickly. More red than yellow should be used.

A sketch can be made with very thin paint. The paper is placed lengthwise; the tiger fills the whole area.

This work was done in the fourth grade (nine to ten years).
It is the purpose of the theoretical exercise to develop awareness of the degrees of intensity in colors.

Similar Subjects: evening sun / switchback / aquarium / balloon woman / wreath of flowers / decorative works / a village by night / dragon / a choir of angels / pheasant / a view from a window at night / fruit / gladioli / goldfish / city at night / cock / harlequin / autumnal fruit / in front of the fire / a witch's house / gates of heavan / Indian / initials / jaguar / jewelry / merry-go-round / stained glass window / crab / lighthouse / bookmark / the fall of Lucifer / mask / a city under the sea / moon and stars / night / fruit / ornament / Easter eggs / palaces at night / parrot / paradise / boa constrictor / Robinson Crusoe / snake / butterfly / jewelry / sunset / church steeple / design for embroidery / carpet / dream picture / monster / circus.

Poster Colors IX. Batik Painting with Poster Colors on Paper: A Sunflower

Materials   Sponge; water jar; palette; sable brush; pencil; eraser; candle; sheet of light-colored paper, about 14 inches by 10 inches; possibly cans and Primus stove.

Subject   The lesson starts with a short introductory talk pointing out the characteristic features of the subject. The sunflower shines brightly like the sun. The flaming petals surround a dark center formed of kernels (dots). The leaves are large, dark green, and heart-shaped. The stems are thick and strong.

Technique   The children first make a pencil drawing in clear, vigorous outlines, with the paper upright. Then the sheet is turned over and held against a window pane. The drawing will show through and can be traced with the candle in thick lines. Finer lines can be drawn with the edge of the candle.

An alternative method is to apply fluid wax with a brush, heating it in a can.

The paper will absorb no color in the waxed places. The paint is applied in a thin consistency with a sable brush. The waxed areas will remain white.

All colors are at our disposal. We begin with the lighter colors. Oil crayons applied thickly could be used instead of wax, thus producing a colored drawing.

The example shown was done in the f o u r t h grade (nine to ten years).

Similar Subjects: apple tree / aquarium / artist / artic regions / station / fortress / clown / dragon / squirrel / lizard / jackdaw / angel / Eskimo / factory / bicycle / fern / pheasant / fish / fish in nets / lilac / fruit / goose / vegetable stall / Puss in Boots / giraffe / goldfish / city / harbor / cock / hare / grasshopper / a witch's house / gates of heaven / chicken / dog / hedgehog / Indian / jewelry / cage / cacti / calendar / cathedral / screech owl / chervil / stained glass window / crab / crocodile / leopard / bookmark / dragonfly / dandelion / corncob / mask / church / daffodil / native huts / hippopotamus / oasis / Easter eggs / palace / palm / parrot / peacock / robber / caterpillar / rain / rhythmical exercises / boa constrictor / Robinson Crusoe / tortoise / snake / butterfly / squirrel / snail shell / snow flake / sea horse / cobweb / town / star / carpet / tiger / tropical island / jungle / bird / Christmas tree / wild duck / winter / robot / magic gardens.

C. Decorative Painting

Not only can painting stand on its own merits, but it can also serve to decorate objects. In the latter case, it has to be adapted to another material and be subordinate to its plastic and technical qualities. A few decorative-painting techniques are given below.

I. Paste Engravings

Materials Distemper, wallpaper paste, or any paste soluble in water; bristle brush; large sheets of non-absorbent wrapping paper, well pasted; several pieces of cardboard; nails; scissors; comb; knitting needles.

Technique The colors are mixed with a little water in a can. The paste should have a thin, fluid consistency. Poster colors can be used instead of distemper.

a) The desks are covered with newspaper. The paste is spread with a piece of cardboard; then we paint into the pasted ground with well-diluted color. The design should be decorative rather than pictorial. Ornamental motifs can be scratched or scraped into the ground with simple tools such as nails, knitting needles, a comb, the edge of a card, etc. The light paper ground will show through again. The work is completed while the paste is wet.

Brushes and other tools must be well cleaned after use. This is a decorative medium suitable for book covers and all ornamental purposes.

b) The paint is mixed with paste and then spread over the sheet of paper in the ratio of 1 part of paste to 4 parts of color mixture.

We paint freely with hands and fingers, letting the mixture drip on to the paper, drawing shapes out of the blots and splotches. The important thing is a relaxed and unconstrained activity, although the result may not turn out to be a work of art.

c) Blot pictures excite the imagination of the children. The pasted and painted paper is folded down the middle, both halves being pressed together and separated again (starting from one corner). Both paint and paste must be wet. Blotting can also be done by splashing and spraying color on to the pasted ground, folding the sheet, and separating it as above. Or a second sheet can be placed over the first pasted and painted sheet and pulled off, leaving behind a texture. Blot pictures can, of course, also be done with ink or poster color on plain paper.

d) The ground is prepared with rather thick paste and drawn on with ink or drawing ink.

II. Painting on Ceramic Tiles. A Goat

Materials   Two unglazed bathroom tiles per child, one of which is used for a free subject; sable brush; water jar; ceramic paints; sponge.

Technique   The shape of the animal is left as a white space, and only the dark background is painted. We begin with a pencil sketch; erasers are not allowed.
The goat should be as large as possible. Ceramic paints come in sticks and jars. The sticks are used for linear drawing. The tiles are wetted with the sponge before the color is applied.
An alternative method is first to paint the whole tile and to scratch out the drawing afterwards. The tiles have to be fired and glazed in a pottery; they can then be used as table mats.

The example shown was done in the first grade (six to seven years).

Similar Subjects: purely decorative designs on tiles / ant / blackbird / artist / aster / bear / bee / flower / buffalo / clown / dragon / lizard / polar bear / duck / Eskimo / owl / pheasant / fish / heron / flamingo / frog / fox / goose / Puss in Boots / ferns / cock / harlequin / grasshopper / stag / chicken / dog / hedgehog / initials / red currant / beetle / camel / rabbit / cat / screech owl / crane / crocodile / cow / leopard / dragonfly / lion / locomotive / ladybird / marten / mask / mouse / sea gull / man in the moon / marmot / daffodil / rhinoceros / ornament / panther / parrot / peacock / horse / prince / princess / raven / caterpillar / deer / rider / reindeer / boa constrictor / chessboard / sheep / tortoise / snail / snowflake / swallow / sea horse / stork / pigeon / tiger / birds / ram / weasel / wolf / zebra / circus.

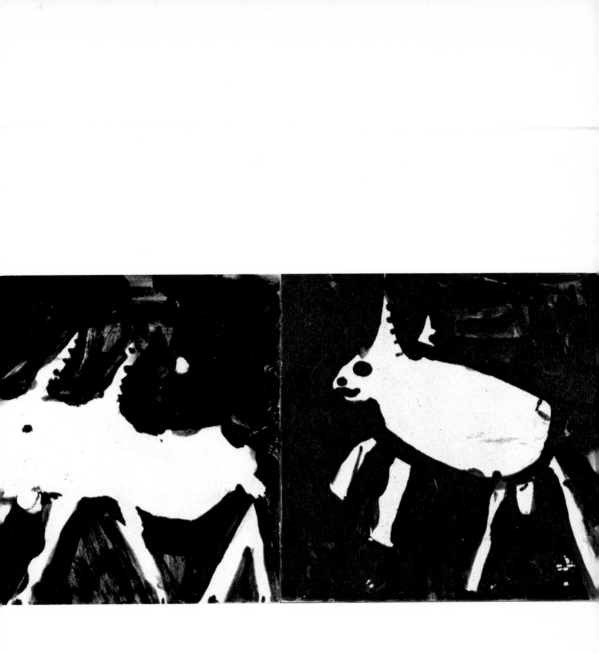

III. Painting on Paper or Wooden Boxes

Decorative painting is best practiced on objects which by their very nature demand decoration. The decoration must not, however, infringe upon the formal character of the object.

Materials   Handmade folded boxes, cigar boxes, or round wooden boxes (about 6 inches in diameter); poster colors; sponge; water jar; palette; bristle and sable brushes; ruler; pencil; eraser; compasses; varnish.

Technique   The box is rubbed down with glass paper. Lid and sides are painted neatly either in a very light or a very dark color. The lid may be light and the sides dark, or vice versa. Allow the box to dry. The lid and sides are decorated in two separate processes.

For the lid we choose ornamental forms which fit into the circle (concentric or radial) and motifs which are easily carried out with the brush—like simple dots, dashes, and dabs (see page 14)—using a clear design of alternate lines and areas.

The decoration on the box should harmonize with that on the sides of the lid. The sides of the box are best left in one color. The decoration on the sides and the top of the lid should consist of variations of the same motif.

The color scheme should be restricted, with emphasis on a strong tonal contrast. Finally, the outside of the box is given a coat of colorless varnish.

Large wooden boxes can be decorated in the same manner.

The examples shown were made by children in the third grade (eight to nine years).

IV. Painting Easter Eggs

Materials   Poster colors; sable brush; sponge; water jar; Easter eggs; wire egg-holders.

Technique   We apply the usual poster color technique. In choosing the decoration, the shape of the eggs has to be taken into consideration.

Crosses and stars are suitable for top and base; rays spread from one end. Horizontal or upright stripes are interspersed with simple motifs (see page 14).

Easter eggs can also be decorated in batik (see page 94).

V. Under Glass Painting

Materials   Colored chalks or poster colors; sable brush; sponge; water jar; palette; pane of glass, about 12 inches by 8 inches.

Technique   A chalk drawing is made directly on the glass. The color is applied thickly. The painted side of the glass is backed by a sheet of white, black, or silver paper according to the desired effect. The brightness of the colors is greatly enhanced by the glass.

The best way of using poster colors under glass is to make a colored brush drawing with the sable brush, taking care not to touch paint which has already dried. Here, too, the work is backed by white or colored paper. This technique is very suitable for Christmas subjects.

D. Cutting, Tearing, and Pasting Techniques

Cutting and tearing paper offers innumerable possibilities which can easily be combined. The essential technical points are explained here. This kind of work forms a valuable supplement to drawing and painting.

I. Folding Cut

Materials Gummed colored paper; small pointed scissors; several paper napkins; pieces of paper in postcard size; sheets of newspapers.

Technique The paper is first folded and then cut. To practice we first cut several squares out of newspaper. We fold the first square once down the middle and cut out small shapes along the edges (squares, oblongs, triangles, flames, stripes, crosses, spirals). Shapes cut into the folded edge will be doubled.

The second square is folded twice. Shapes are cut out of both folded edges.

The third square can be folded several times, parallel to one edge (accordian-fashion), or once or twice diagonally. Shapes can also be cut out a circle or a hexagon.

The results should be pinned on the blackboard for comparison.

The same exercise is now repeated with colored paper.

The basic shapes of the decorations for postcards should be 1^1/$_2$ to 2 inches, for napkins 3^1/$_2$ to 4 inches.

The folding cut can be backed with different colors or cut out of two kinds of paper, one of which is stuck behind the other, overlapping slightly.

Stylized plant motifs, snowflakes, or silhouettes of people and animals decorated in folding cut present further possibilities.

The examples shown were done in the s e c o n d grade (seven to eight years). The folding cut can be practiced throughout the primary grades.

This technique is very suitable for all decorative purposes such as designs for wrapping paper, bookmarks, invitation cards, etc.

II. Silhouettes. Shepherds in the Field (A Group Project)

The silhouette, originally cut only from black paper, can now be cut from any paper. The choice of subject should, however, be restricted to clearly outlined shapes. The scissor cut must not be untidy, because it represents the essential shape of a figure. It forces us to cut directly and to concentrate on our work.
A preliminary sketch would spoil the tension and the surprise effects of the process. The result would be a cut-out drawing, but not a characteristic silhouette. The scissor cut is very suitable for group pictures. It can be practiced throughout the primary grades.

Materials Gummed colored paper; a variety of colored paper, such as magazines, catalogues, wallpaper, etc.; small pointed scissors; glue; sheet of paper, about 60 inches by 20 inches, in a neutral color like gray or beige.

Subject The lesson begins with a short introductory talk pointing out all the details of the figures. The bearded shepherds wear coats and hats, hooded capes, etc., and carry sticks and lanterns; they might stand, kneel, or sit. The sheep have round noses, small ears, thick woolly bodies, tails, and thin legs.

Technique We begin with a shepherd. Every child is given a piece of colored paper, about 8 inches by 5 inches.
The children should be shown how to cut carefully without any preliminary drawing. They must not forget anything, for once a piece is cut out, it is irrevocably lost. The shepherd is cut out in one piece, including hair, nose, beard, fingers, and shoelaces. It is advisable to cut in large areas (head, body, legs, etc.), putting in the detail later. The figure is shown in profile, The completed scissor cut can be livened up with two or three decorative features in different colors (belt, collar, hat, etc.). Or the folding cut can be employed to add bits of decoration (lanterns, borders on the edge of the coat, etc.). The figure is pressed inside a book. Care should be taken to move the hand holding the paper while cutting, and **not** the scissors. Every child then cuts out a sheep, not forgetting the bell and woolly fleece (about 6 inches by 7 inches).
With the help of the whole class, all finished scissor cuts are then arranged on the large sheet of paper and finally glued down.

This composition was done in the t h i r d grade (eight to nine years).

Similar subjects: Ali Baba and the 40 Thieves / aquarium / artists / automobiles / bunch of flowers / flowering twig / herd of buffalo / a troupe of clowns / David and Goliath / railway / ice hockey match / angel / factory / family outing / haul of fish / frog / football / the goose girl / Puss in Boots / giraffe / goldfish / harbor / cock / harlequin / witch / stag / wedding / dog / Indian / fun fair / cage with animals / camel ride / the battle of the knights / merry-go-round / cat / the three wise men from the East / crab / crocodile / lion / rabble / ladybird / sea gull / oasis / panther / peacock / horse racing / cycle racing / robber / rider on horseback / knight / Robinson Crusoe / Little Red Ridinghood / story of creation / soldiers / Santa Claus / devil / national costumes / moving house / cattle market / wood / magic garden / circus / zoo.

III. Transparencies. The Seven Dwarfs

This medium is reminiscent of stained-glass painting. Instead of glass we use transparent colored paper, and instead of lead mounting, strips of cardboard. Unlike the preceding technique, we cut out separate parts of a figure which are joined afterwards. The light shining through brightens the colors. Transparent pictures can be produced without cardboard strips by joining the edges of the colored paper, sticking one over the other. Four transparent pictures can be made into a lantern or a lamp shade.

Materials   Transparent colored paper; scissors; razor blade with a cork handle or paper knife; pencil; light poster colors; sable brush; eraser; glue; black cardboard, about 14 inches by 10 inches.

Subject   The children are told to include numerous details, such as tree trunks, mushrooms, stones, grass, sun or moon and stars, forest animals, etc., in the composition.

Technique   We begin by creating a cardboard framework. This is done with a simple linear brush drawing (lines about ¼ inch thick), using light poster color.

The work can be placed upright or lengthwise. All lines hang together like the threads of a net. Very small shapes and bent lines are to be avoided, because they are difficult to cut out. The spaces between the lines are cut away with a razor blade or a paper knife, leaving a cardboard framework.

The shapes cut out of colored paper are then fitted into the spaces. Their size must allow for the cardboard edges. Colors can be toned up or down or mixed by using double layers of colored paper. The edges are fastened to the cardboard strips with very little glue. Colored papers must not project into adjoining areas.

The smaller areas are put in first to give the children confidence.

The example shown was done in the fourth grade (nine to ten years).

Similar Subjects: apple tree / aquarium / artist / bunch of asters / bathing scene / flowers / botanical gardens / clown / cathedral / the palace of Sleeping Beauty / lizard / angel / owl / pheasant / fish / fishing port / goose girl / goldfish / harbor / cock / harlequin / witch's house / gates of heaven / shepherds in the fields / wedding coach / Indian / Joseph and Mary / merry-go-round / chestnut blossom / screech owl / the three wise men from the East / mask / man in the moon / church / nightingale / oasis / fruit-picking / parrot / paradise / peacock / rider on horseback / boa constrictor / knight / Robinson Crusoe / Little Red Ridinghood / butterfly / story of creation / swimming / spider / pinewood / national costumes / tropical island / jungle / wood / Christmas scene / the goblins / magic gardens / circus.

IV. Torn-Paper Pictures. An Owl

Colored paper is torn into little pieces. The colors are carefully chosen; the shape is less important. A motif is composed out of the piece. This technique is suitable throughout the primary grades; it is a valuable loosening exercise. Distinguishing features are the soft joints and the mosaic-like character of the forms.

Materials   Colored paper (all grays, ocher, and brown); glue; sheet of dark paper, about 14 inches by 10 inches.

Subject   We begin by tearing paper into bits of various shapes and sizes unrelated to the theme, which is then explained in detail: the owl has a large head, round protruding eyes, a pointed, hooked beak, and a soft, freckled and striped plumage.

Technique   No preliminary sketch is made. The children are shown how to arrange the feathers like the scales of a fish; this can be done very easily with the torn pieces of paper. A little glue is applied to every piece. The larger pieces are used first and the smaller ones stuck over them. The result should resemble plumage. Shape and color must co-ordinate. Emphasis will be on the two-dimensional character of the work. Finally, the picture is pressed.
Further tearing exercises:
A silhouette is torn out and decorated with bits of paper.
Parts are torn out of a shape, thus forming a pattern.
A shape can be changed by inserting torn shapes.
Torn shapes can be backed completely or partly with paper of a different color.

The example shown was done in the fourth grade (nine to ten years).

Similar Subjects: evening sun / monkey / blackbird / artist / asters / bear / bee / flowers / flowering tree / buffalo / clown / dahlia / the palace of Sleeping Beauty / squirrel / lizard / polar bear / jackdaw / duck / Eskimo / pheasant / spotted salamander / fish / flamingo / bat / fox / goose / ghost / vegetable stall / Puss in Boots / goldfish / cock / hamster / harlequin / hare / harvest time / autumn / witch / stag / shepherd and his flock / chicken / bumblebee / dog / Indian Chief / jaguar / camel / animals fighting / rabbit / chestnut / blossom / cat / crane / cow / deciduous tree / leopard / dragonfly / lion / sea gull / man in the moon / marmot / marten / nightingale / daffodil / native hut / carnation / oasis / ornament / desert island / panther / parrot / crow / caterpillar / reindeer / Robinson Crusoe's island / Little Red Ridinghood / a flock of sheep / snake / butterfly / swallow / swan / sun / sunflower / pansy / stork / fir tree / pigeon / carpet / devil / tiger / tropical island / moving house / jungle / violet / birds / woods / aquatic birds / ram / weasel / wild duck / winter / wolf / cloud / magic gardens / zebra / goat / gypsy / circus / zoo.

V. Paper and Fabric Cut (Appliqué). Bird of Paradise (Fabric)

The cutout can lead on to paper and fabric appliqué. Parts of the desired shape are pieced together to form a whole.

Bits of paper and hand-colored paper of every kind can be used to allow each child to choose his individual color scheme. For fabric appliqué we use patterned and plain-colored cloth samples, etc. Torn shapes will have a softer quality than cut ones.

The chief attraction of this medium lies in the interplay of color, pattern, and texture.

Both types of appliqué are suitable throughout the primary grades.

Materials Gummed and ungummed colored paper for paper appliqué; patterned and plain colored cloth samples for fabric appliqué; string, thread, scissors, glue; the ground (14 inches by 10 inches) is prepared the day before with poster colors; strong paper or cardboard.

Subject This subject must not be described in detail, for the children should invent the bird from their imagination. A story might stimulate the younger children.

Technique To achieve a uniform effect, it is advisable to use either paper or fabric entirely.

The ground can be placed upright or lengthwise; the bird fills the whole sheet. No preliminary drawing is made. The shapes are stuck down as soon as they are cut out. We start with the largest shapes. Arrangement, color, and texture are left entirely to the children.

Texture and structure of the fabric should be pointed out to the children. Fabric appliqué can be varied further by sewing and embroidering on it. The paper for paper appliqué can be cut or torn.

The example shown was done in the t h i r d grade (eight to nine years).

Similar Subjects: monkey / ant / blackbird / asters / automobile / baker / bathing scene / station / building site / flowers / beehive / Tom Thumb / David and Goliath / lizard / railway / strawberry plant stem / my family / at the photographer's / factory / spotted salamander / fish / lilac / forsythia / frog / football team / garden / gardener / vegetable stall / goldfish / a gentleman / autumnal tree / hedgehog / initials / beetle / calendar / chimney sweep / crab / crocodile / tree / dragonfly / bookmark / dandelion / locomotive / ladybird / mask / army / nightingale / daffodil / hippopotamus / oasis / fruit-picking / palace / peacock / robber / rider on horseback / giant / knight / Robinson Crusoe / tortoise / snake / cowslip / butterfly / snail / story of creation / educational trip / gladiolus / swimming / self-portrait / soldiers / sunflower / at the seashore / dance / tropical island / gymnast / jungle / violet / forget-me-not / Christmas / winter / magic gardens / tent / circus / zoo / dwarf.

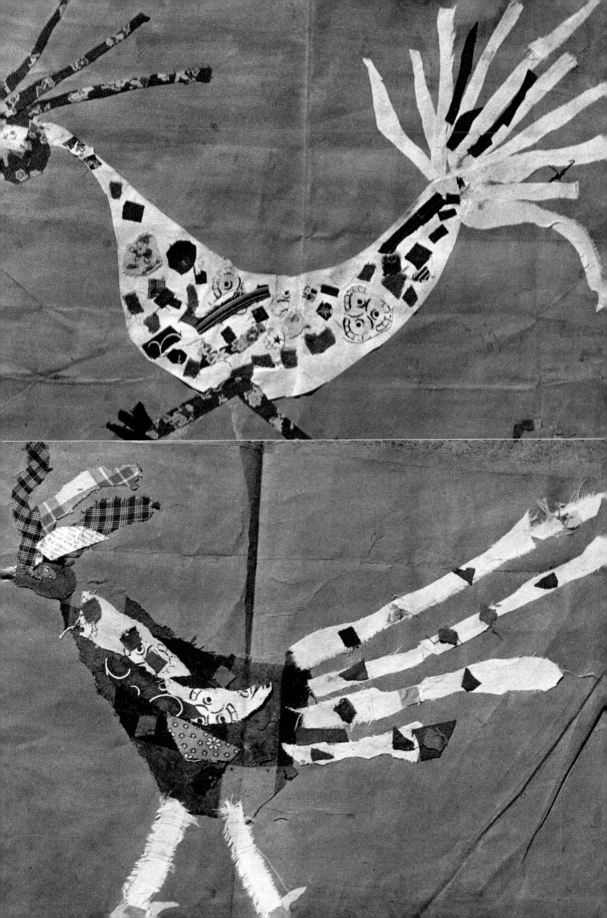

VI. Collage. Fishing Port

Collage is a cutting and glueing technique. Torn paper shapes, cutouts, and silhouettes are combined in this method. The problem here is to discover forms in bits of torn paper which can be used for the set theme. This ability to integrate can not be expected before the fourth grade (nine to ten years).

Materials   Colored-paper remnants; scissors; glue; pencil; handcolored ground of strong paper, about 6 inches by 8 inches.
We let the children cut and tear numerous shapes of every kind and size (regular, irregular, long, thin, etc.) without divulging the subject matter. The scissors are then laid aside.

Subject   The subject is explained in detail: the haphazard arrangement of the many boats in a harbor, the different types and shapes of boats. Describe the fittings: sails—which can be triangular, square, taut or slack—masts, ropes, flags, nets, etc. There should be slight movement in the water.

Technique   We employ a free combination of tearing, cutting, and silhouette techniques. The ground can be placed lengthwise or upright, representing the sea. We work from background to foreground. Most of the required shapes are probably among the bits of paper; others are composed of several bits. Large shapes are stuck down first. The boats must be well spaced to achieve clarity. Scissors are used only when the desired form cannot be found or made up at all. Finally, the pictures are pressed.

The example shown was done in the fourth grade (nine to ten years).

Similar Subjects: switchback / the sale / traffic / railroad station / balloon woman / building site / beehive / botanical gardens / bookmark / clown / cathedral / railway / icebergs / jackdaw / factory / carnival / football player / vegetable stall / city / harlequin / building of houses / autumnal wood / a witch's house / gates of heaven / skyscraper / chicken house / wigwams / merry-go-round / shop / dandelion / market / man from Mars / machine / church / North Pole / oasis / palaces / parrot / lake dwellings / peacock / boa constrictor / a knight's castle / Robinson Crusoe's hut / a flock of sheep / castle / butterfly / sailing regatta / sunflower / town / pine wood / carpet / designs for place cards / tiger / national costume display / jungle / forest / wash day / wharf / windmill / winter / skyscraper city / robot / magic garden / circus.

VII. Metal Foil. Christmas Tree Decorations

For Christmas decorations we use metal foil which is colored on both sides. The material can be cut easily with scissors, bent, rolled up, folded, or scratched.

Materials   Colored foil (gold, silver, copper, ocher, red, blue, green); scissors; pencil; ruler; knitting needle.

Technique   The children begin by making a star. Every child is handed a 4-inch square of gold foil on which a circle 4 inches in diameter has been drawn with the compass (a). An inner circle is drawn by hand (b).

With a pencil we then sketch a zigzag line with pointed teeth (c) or square teeth (d) along the outer border so that the indentations are of equal depth. The inner circle is decorated with simple motifs, engraved with the knitting needle (e).

The tip of each point is then rolled over a pencil.

Finally, a hole is pierced and the star is hung up by a colored thread.

For a chain of colored foil, we cut strips of equal size (a), 4 inches long and ³/₄ inch wide. Both ends are joined (b). The end is folded twice (c). This fastening is pressed tight with the finger, and the inside of the link is molded into a round shape (d). Each of the following links must be hooked into the preceding one before it is fastened. It is best to decorate the strips when they are still flat. The chains are hung on the Christmas tree either open or closed.

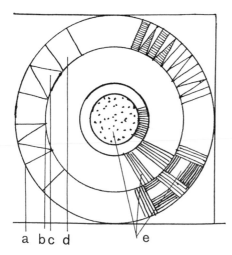

a b c d   e

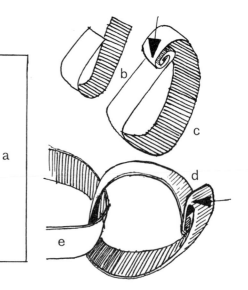

E. Printing Techniques

We distinguish between three types of printing processes: intaglio or deep printing (etching, copper engraving), relief or high printing (stamp linocut, woodcut), and planographic or flat printing (lithography).

In intaglio, the areas to be printed are incised below the nonprinting surface. In relief the areas to be printed are raised above the nonprinting areas; the areas not to be printed are cut away. In planographic printing, printing and nonprinting areas remain flat.

Whenever blocks or plates are used, a large number of prints can be made. This ability to reproduce is the important aspect of manual printing techniques. Only a few of these techniques are suitable for the primary grades.

Nothing develops the sense of the expressive possibilities of black and white more acutely than work with printing blocks. The active white contrasts clearly against the passive black. Children grasp in a simple way the technique of print-making and reproduction processes. They are forced to grapple with form. Only themes with a graphic character should be chosen.

I. Plaster Engraving. Printing a Line Drawing from a Plaster Plate: A Giant

Materials   About ³/₄ pound of plaster per child; the lid of a cardboard box, about 6 inches square; tools for incising (nail, needle, engraving tools); poster color; brush or sponge; printing ink; a sheet of glass; roller; spatula; newsprint.

Subject   The subject is a giant who roams the woods with his bow and arrow.

Technique   We make a plaster plate by pouring thin liquid plaster (for mixing plaster see page 145) into the cardboard box lid to a thickness of about ¹/₂ inch. When the plaster has dried, the cardboard base is detached. Uneven parts of the surface are rubbed down with glass paper. The plaster plate is then colored with a layer of thin poster paint, ink, or drawing ink, using a brush or a sponge.

The drawing is scratched into the plate; it may be sketched in pencil first. The format is upright, the figure filling the whole space.

It is easier to scratch out linear forms than to scrape out whole areas. Dots, dashes, and dabs are easily done. The finest trace of an incised line will appear in print; it must, however, be ¹/₁₆ inch deep.

Lines not deep enough will full up with ink and consequently will blot. Corrections can only be made on shallow lines by incising them deeper and wider.

The plates should be inked by the instructor. The consistency of the ink must be rich and not too fluid. The paper is placed over the plate, leaving a margin of equal width all around. The paper is rubbed with the fingernail, separated from the plate (starting from one corner), and left to dry.

Several prints should be taken, because not every print will be of good quality.

Finally, the plaster plate can be hung on the wall. The drawing should be retouched for this purpose. A hole in the back will allow it to be hung on a short nail.

Alternative printing surfaces are slate, strong cardboard, and linoleum. The drawing is made with a nail in slate, a knitting needle in cardboard, and a gouge in linoleum. The printing process is the same.

For under-glass etching, a sheet of glass is covered thickly with black poster paint. The drawing is scratched into the dry paint (lines, areas, texture). The work is backed with white, colored, or glossy paper and mounted on a piece of cardboard, edged with strong tape.

The example shown was done in the first grade (six to seven years).

Similar Subjects (see also pen drawing, page 30): monkey / ant / blackbird / apple tree / aquarium / Noah's ark / artist / automobile / railroad station / bear / building site / bee / bunch of flowers / botanical gardens / boxer / buffalo / clown / lady / thistle / village / dragon / lizard / railway / ice hockey player / angel / duck / owl / factory / fern / pheasant / fish / haul of fish / bat / frog / fox / football player / garden / ghost / Puss in Boots / giraffe / cock / harlequin / hare / grasshopper / witch / stag / chicken / bumblebee / dog / hedgehog / Indian / the hunter / cage with animals / camel / cathedral / cat / screech owl / chervil / crane / crab / crocodile / cow / leopard / dragonfly / lion / dandelion / machine / sea gull / fruit harvest / palm trees / peacock / horse / prince / princess / cycle racing / robber / rider / reindeer / giant / boa constrictor / knight / Robinson Crusoe / sheep / tortoise / snail / sea horse / soldiers / sunflower / spider / sportsman / Santa Claus / bull / fir tree / dance / tiger / jungle / birds / plantain / Christmas tree / robot / magic gardens / zebra / goat / circus / dwarf.

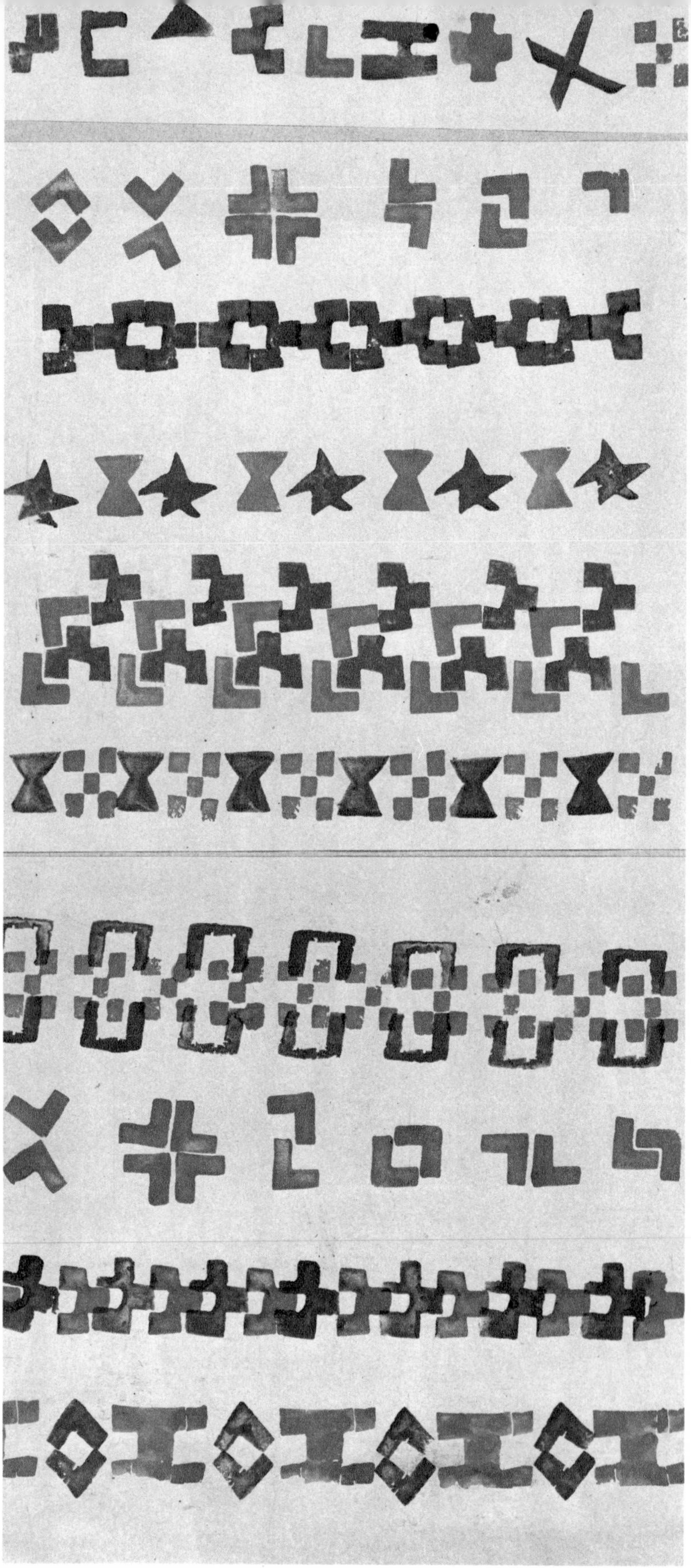

II. Potato and Rubber Stamps. Patterns

Printing with a stamp is the easiest of the raised printing techniques. Shapes are cut out of potatoes, bits of rubber, or cork. These are used as motifs or pieced together to form a design. Suitable printing surfaces are paper, cloth, or hessian. This simple printing technique can be practiced as early as the first grade.

Materials 2 or 3 firm, raw, washed potatoes; pieces of cork and rubber; 2 or 3 poster colors; pocket knife; brush; 3 or 4 sheets of absorbent white or colored paper, about 14 inches by 10 inches; palette; water jar; sponge; newspaper; blotting paper.

Technique 1. Printing with potato stamps. The potato is cut in half. We cut ornamental motifs out of graph paper, put them on the potato, and cut round the shape. The stamp should be about $1/2$ inch high. The rest of the potato is used as a stamp grip. The decorative shapes (squares, circles, triangles, stars, crosses, etc.) are cut directly out of the block ($1^1/4$ inches square). After cutting several blocks, we dry the surface with blotting paper and rub it with turpentine.

The color is now spread on the palette and mixed with very little water, thus providing an inkpad or applied to the block with a brush. The block is tested on the edge of a sheet of newspaper.

We print first a decorative border in one color and then combine several motifs and different colors.

Blocks of equal or different sizes can be used in a variety of ways: aligned, scattered, interlocked, etc.

This technique is a good preparation for the linocut.

The blocks are also suitable for fabric printing, if fabric printing inks are used.

2. For printing with a rubber stamp, see page 132.

The example was done in the first grade (six to seven years).

Similar Subjects: leaf of an album / writing paper / envelopes / bookbinding / decorative designs / invitation cards / gift-wrapping paper / greeting cards / notebook cover / book labels / initials / design for a necklace / calendar / bookmark / wallpaper, curtains, bedspread, carpet, tablecloth / menu / time table / towel / place cards / Christmas wrapping paper.

III. Linocut Printing. An Owl

The basis of this graphic technique is the tension between black and white. Every white line or area must be balanced by an equivalent value in black. The child will sense this demand at once. Potato stamps, silhouettes, and brush drawings are important preparations. Experience shows that better results are obtained when the technique is tackled immediately, without allowing time for practice. The pupil has to conquer every new technique for himself. When the small dimensions of the stamp become insufficient, we turn to the linocut. In the primary grades we work only with small blocks (4 inches by 6 inches to 6 inches by 8 inches).
Linocut printing is suitable from the second grade on. Subjects should have a strongly graphic and two-dimensional character.

Materials   Plain-colored linoleum with even surface, 7 inches by 6 inches and ¹/₂ inch thick; well-sharpened pocket knife or special linoleum-cutting tools; printing inks; poster colors; spatula; roller; sheet of glass; newspapers; newsprint.

Subject   The lesson begins with a short introductory talk pointing out the details of the subject. The owl has big shining eyes, a hooked beak, rings around the eyes which make it look as if it were wearing glasses, small ears and a plumage made up of dabs and dashes.

Technique   a) Cutting

The cutting principle is the same as for the potato stamp. All nonprinting areas are cut away. The V-gouge is used to cut lines and the U-gouge to scrape out areas (white or textured).
Shapes which are left untouched will appear completely black in print. The knife must be held as flat as possible and away from us to avoid injury.
The V-gouge can be used for creating texture; it will chip out little bits of lino (dots, dabs, dashes).
There are various technical possibilities. The white line is cut out, the gouge leaving a V-shaped track. The black line is left standing; in this case, areas on either side have to be cut away, so that the result will be an inverted V. Areas and texture are obtained similarly.
Straight lines and shapes are easier to cut than curved ones. The work must be done carefully and systematically, without preliminary drawing.
Corrections can only be made by cutting away more material; nothing can be added. The aim is a decorative rather than a naturalistic or dramatic effect. Designs in brush drawing on paper or—more suitable for smaller children—on the linoleum itself will strengthen the feeling for black and white balance.
The print reverses left to right; some objects may therefore have to be cut in their mirror image.

b) Printing

We spread a little printing ink over the glass with the spatula and roll it out. Cleanliness is most important for good printing results. The spatula and roller are put down on the edge of the inked surface. It is advisable that the instructor ink the blocks.

The block is placed on a sheet of newspaper which is exchanged for a clean sheet after every rolling.

The most suitable paper for printing is newsprint. Thick or rough paper must be dampened first (put between sheets of damp newspaper).

The paper is placed quickly over the inked block with an equal margin all round (about 1 ³/₄ inch). The paper is rubbed well, first with the fingers, then with the palm of the hand, and finally with the handle of the gouge or a spoon (rub-printing as opposed to printing with a press).

A corner is lifted to see how the color is being absorbed. When the result appears satisfactory, the paper is pulled off and left to dry.

If the print turns out very faint, the color was applied too sparsely or the mixture was too thick; if the color has run into the lines, it was too liquid. Several prints are possible.

The tools must be cleaned thoroughly, first with newspaper and then with rags and turpentine. The knives must be sharpened from time to time.

Colored prints can be made with poster colors and lino—or book-printing—colors.

Muliicolored prints are too difficult for the primary grades, since a new block has to be made for every color.

This print was done in the third grade (eight to nine years).

Similar Subjects: monkey / Ali Baba and the 40 Thieves (G) / blackbird / apple tree / aquarium (G) / Noah's ark animals (G) / artist / automobile / railroad station / bear / building site / bee / bunch of flowers / flowering twig / flowering tree / botanical gardens / boxer / buffalo / fortress / clown / dahlia / David and Goliath / thistle / cathedral / village / Sleeping Beauty / dragon / squirrel / lizard / elephant / jackdaw / duck / donkey / Eskimo / owl / factory / pheasant / at the window / fish / flamingo / frog / fox / goose / garden / Puss in Boots / giraffe / greeting cards / harbor / cock / harlequin / a gentleman / witch / stag / shepherd / wedding coach / chicken / dog / hedgehog / Indian / industrial town / jaguar / beetle / calendar (G) / chimney sweep / rabbit / cat / king and queen on their thrones / cow / teacher / leopard / lion / locomotive / ladybird / mask / sea gull / man in the moon / marmot / marten / nightingale / daffodil / rhinoceros / Neptune / hippopotamus / panther / parrot / peacock / horse / prince / princess / crow / rider on horseback / reindeer / giant / Robinson Crusoe / sheep / tortoise / snake / snail / swallow / swan / sailboat / tightrope-walker / sunflower / sport / Santa Claus / bull / stork / pigeon / animals (G) / tiger / jungle (detail) / birds / fir tree / ram / weasel / wild duck / winter / wolf / magician / zebra / goat / circus / zoo / dwarf.

IV. Cardboard Printing

The cardboard cut is a particularly simple and cheap printing technique. A silhouette cut out of cardboard serves as a printing block.

Materials   Strong, not too thick cardboard; scissors; printing ink; roller; spatula; pane of glass; spoon; newsprint, 4 to 5 sheets of about 12 inches by 8 inches per child.

Technique   The block is cut out of the cardboard. The subject should be graphic and two-dimensional (see page 117).

The block is placed on newspaper and the ink rolled over as for a linocut. Newsprint or tissue paper will be found particularly suitable.

The paper is then rubbed over the block and pulled off. Thick or rough paper must again be put between sheets of damp newspaper.

Tools must be cleaned thoroughly.

V. Stencil Printing. A Cockerel

Stencil printing is a variant of cardboard printing. The motif is cut as a negative shape out of cardboard or used as a stencil (positive). This technique is employed for special grouping (alignment, scattering) and overlapping.

Materials   Poster colors; brush or roller; palette; water jar; printing paper or fabric; knife; scissors; razor blade or paper knife; strong cardboard or special stencil card; newspapers.

Subject   For details of the subject, see page 16.

Technique   The size of the stencil should be at least 3 inches by 2 inches; smaller shapes would be difficult to cut out. The figure is sketched in outline.

The positive stencil is in the form of a silhouette. Drawings can be made inside the figure.

The negative stencil is cut away, leaving a sufficiently large frame; drawing within the figure is therefore impossible.

The stencil is soaked in water for a few minutes until soft, and then pressed between newspapers. It is then put over the place which is to be printed. We hold the figure in position with one hand and apply the color with the other, leading the brush toward the outside on the positive stencil and from the outside toward the inside on the negative one. The positive stencil can be inked with the roller.

Different groupings, as well as mirror images, are possible.

The stencil might have to be lifted off the paper with the help of pins.

Positive and negative forms can be used next to, or over, each other.

If we want to use another color, the stencil must be cleaned with a wet sponge.

The stencil technique should be tried only on very simple examples of figurative shapes and ornamental motifs.

Similar Subjects: monkey / ant / blackbird / automobile / bear / flowers / buffalo / writing paper / thistle / dragon / invitation cards / lizard / elephant / pheasant / fish / heron / flamingo / frog / fox / goose / the goose girl / garden / giraffe / greeting cards / gondola / harbor / cock / notebook cover / grasshopper / stag / chicken / dog / insects / beetle / calendar / camel / cat / chervil / king / crab / dragonfly / dandelion / ladybird / mouse / sea gull / daffodil / fruit / palm / peacock / horse / crow / deer / rider on horseback / reindeer / snake / butterfly / snail / swallow / pig / sea horse / spider / stars / bull / printed material / stork / fir tree / pigeon / tiger / birds (G) / wood / aquatic birds / Christmas wrapping paper / zebra / goat / circus (G) / dwarf.

VI. Glass Printing

This technique can be tried with leftover color at the end of a lesson on lino cutting.

Materials   Printing ink; a sheet of glass; roller; spatula; newsprint; pencil; brush.

Technique   The inked glass prepared for the printing of the linocut has dried a little by now. We place a thin sheet of paper or a piece of fabric over it and draw on it with the finger or a pencil. The drawing will appear on the other side.

Another effect can be obtained if every child paints on a piece of glass with different poster colors. This painting is covered with tissue paper and a second protective sheet. The paper is rubbed on with the spoon and finally pulled off. We thus obtain a mirror image.

A further possibility would be to ink the glass and to wipe the drawing out of the color, using the end of a brush handle, a stick, or a cloth. The paper is rubbed on and pulled off as before. Finally, we could color the linocut with a brush, using several colors. This also makes one print.

VII. Fabric Printing

Most of the printing techniques already shown can be used on fabric as well as on paper. Fabric printing, being of interest mainly to girls, can be taught from the fourth grade on in needlework classes.

Materials Stamps; stencils; linocuts; fabric printing inks; newspapers and rags; a pane of glass; roller; spatula; hammer; brush; cotton waste.

Suitable fabrics are raw cotton, jute, silk, raw silk, fine linen.

Technique The colors will appear pure only on fabrics of light and neutral colors. On a colored material we obtain a mixture of the ground color and the color of the ink.

Painting directly on fabric can be regarded as the origin of fabric printing. The technique differs in no way from the ordinary poster color technique. The colors are best mixed with water in little bowls. Only line drawing and effects of texture should be attempted, since large painted areas are apt to smudge.

The glaze of the material has to be washed out in warm water first. The fabric is then stretched, smoothed out, and spread on newspaper.

For smaller motifs we use the stamp (potato, rubber, lino, cork, see page 121), which is first pressed on the well-inked glass and then on to the fabric. The colors should be first tried out on newspapers and on different types of materials.

Linocuts with decorative motifs are combined freely or used to form a repetitive pattern. The linoleum is inked and, by working on it with a hammer, evenly and firmly pressed on to the fabric. Air compressed between layers of newspapers (as many as possible) acts as counter-pressure. We hold the piece of linoleum at two opposite ends to prevent it from moving during hammering. Larger prints can be transferred on to the fabric by standing on them.

Colors can be mixed by printing over immediately.

Printing with stencils is well suited for quick and varied repetitions and accumulations of small forms. There are positive and negative stencils. The use of several colors is possible.

The color is sprayed over the stencil instead of being applied with the brush. We fasten the stencil with pins and rub the color through a coffee-strainer with an old bristle brush (toothbrush). The texture thus created on the cloth will fill out the negative form or surround the positive one. Only uncomplicated outline figures are suitable. This method can, of course, be applied to paper as well.

When the printing is completed, the fabric must be ironed. We cover the ironing board with tissue paper and, provided the colors are quite dry, iron the printed fabric on the wrong side (silk on both sides) until it is also dry. This process is repeated on the right side after it has been dampened with a cloth.

Hand-printed fabrics must not be washed before six weeks, and then only by hand in lukewarm water, using soap flakes.

VIII. Batik Printing

The batik technique originated in Java. It is based on the fact that wax will absorb no color.

Materials Frame (embroidery frame for small pieces of fabric); wax (half beeswax, half candle wax) in tins; bristle and sable brushes; batik colors in powder form; paint bucket; thermometer; primus stove; double saucepan; iron; newspapers; blotting paper; cambric, silk, or other thin fabric.

Technique A few preparations have to be made before we apply the technique. We wash the glaze out of the fabric in lukewarm water. Then we design the motif and transfer it to the cloth if necessary. The cloth must be pinned to the frame with drawing pins until it is quite taut. The wax is melted in a double saucepan, but not boiled.

The design is now drawn in wax on the fabric. The wax must penetrate the cloth. Thick, heavy materials have to be waxed on both sides. The fabric is now dyed, using the lightest color first. Half a pint of water is brought to a boil with half a teaspoonful of cooking salt. Color is then added until the desired tone is achieved, stirring well all the time. By adding cold water the temperature is reduced to 25°. The color is tested on a rag, bearing in mind that colors are more intense in their wet state. The waxed material is first dipped into cold water and creased until the wax shows cracks and splits, then into the lukewarm dye, where it is left for a quarter of an hour. Finally it is taken out, rinsed in cold water, and hung up to dry. This process is repeated for all the other colors.

Finally, the wax must be removed.

The dry fabric is placed between sheets of newspaper and pressed with a very hot iron, until no more wax is absorbed (the newspaper must be changed frequently). Finally, it is ironed on clean blotting paper.

F. Mosaic Techniques

Mosaic should definitely find a place in the curriculum of the primary grades. Mosaics can be composed of pebbles, china, or glass fragments. Shaping stones would be too difficult for small children, though mosaic can also be made with colored paper or dabbed with a flat bristle brush.

To retain the mosaic character in brush, stamp, and paper mosaic, a very small space must be left between each patch of color (never overlay). Outline and simplification, the basis of every mosaic technique, provide new stimuli and stabilize the sense of form. A charcoal sketch is best suited to the broad line created by mosaic.

I. Brush, Stamp, and Paper Mosaic

1. Brush Mosaic

Materials Two or three poster colors; flat bristle brush; water jar; sponge; palette; sheet of white or neutral colored paper, about 14 inches by 10 inches.

Technique Lines, areas, and textures are composed out of color patches, divided by gaps $1/16$ inch wide which represent the pointing of stone mosaic.
The contrast of quality should be applied in this exercise, for we aim at variety of tones within one color (this applies particularly to stone mosaic). See page 90.

2. Stamp Mosaic. An Elephant

Small stamps are made out of old erasers, using part of the eraser as a grip. Potatoes can be substituted for erasers (see page 121).

Materials   Old erasers; knife; poster colors; brush; palette; sponge; water jar; sheets of dark and neutral absorbent paper, about 14 inches to 10 inches.

Subject   The lesson begins with a short introductory talk, pointing out the main features of the elephant. He is of large size, has a trunk, tusks, cabbage-leaf ears, pillar-like legs, and small eyes.

Technique   First, the stamps have to be cut. The color is applied as for potato stamps. Again, the stamps are first tested on the margin of a sheet of newspaper. The format is horizontal; the figure fills the entire sheet.
The outline can be drawn roughly in pencil. The stamp is put down without pressure. Only two or three colors should be used, keeping the gaps between the color patches as narrow as possible. A dark background can be lit up with white. Here, emphasis is on the contrast of light and dark.
Small and large stamps are used alternately. Children will first stamp the outline, then the inner areas and the background.

The example shown was done in the first grade (six to seven years).

Similar Subjects: monkey / Noah's ark animals (G) / asters / railroad station / building site / flowers / buffalo / clown / dahlia / cathedral / village / lizard / invitation cards / duck / owl / pheasant / spotted sala-mander / fish / lilac / forsythia / goose / greeting cards / goldfish / a bird's-eye view of a town / cock / har-lequin / hare / a witch's house / gates of heaven / skyscraper / chicken / hedgehog / Indian / initials / necklace / rabbit / chestnut blossom / cat / screech owl / king / crab / crocodile / deciduous tree / leopard / mask / sea gull / nightingale / rhinoceros / hippopotamus / oasis / palace / palms / parrot / peacock / crow / rider on horseback / reindeer / boa constrictor / tortoise / butterfly / snail / a flight of swallows / sea horse / sailboat / soldier / sunflower / spider / Santa Claus / town / bull / pinewood / pigeon / carpet / tiger / bird / wood / ram / wild duck / skyscraper / magic gardens / zebra / goat / circus people / dwarf.

3. Paper Mosaic

Paper mosaic is composed of previously cut-out bits of colored or hand-painted paper. The very abundance of color will demand some kind of scheme.

Materials   Colored paper; scissors; glue; dark or neutral ground, about 14 inches by 10 inches.

Technique   The colored paper is cut into pieces of various shapes and sizes. An outline drawing is then made in charcoal, and the pieces of paper are stuck down, leaving a minimum of space between each. Colors should be chosen carefully. The children work from the center or one of the mar-gins along the entire width of the paper.
A larger paper mosaic provides a suitable theme for a group picture.

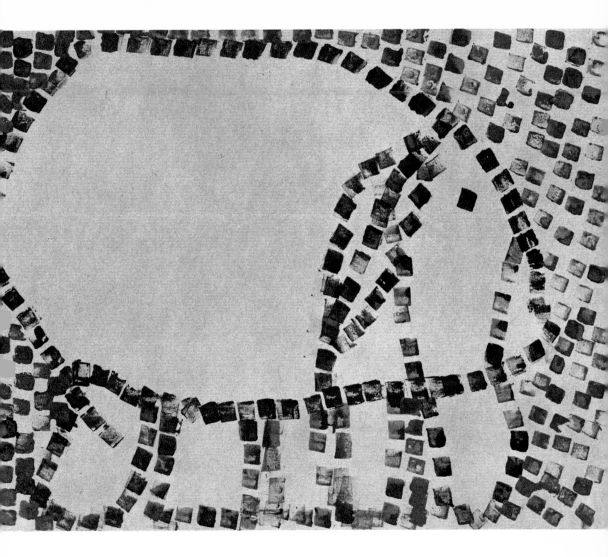

II. Pebble Mosaic. Duck

Colored pebbles of appropriate shapes and sizes can be made into mosaic. Cutting stones is too laborious for younger children, and ready-cut stones are too expensive.

Materials An assortment of attractive pebbles; the lid of a cardboard box, about 12 inches by 8 inches and 1 inch deep; 1 pound of clay; 2 to 3 pounds of builders' plaster or cement per child; pencil.

Subject The lesson begins with a brief introductory talk pointing out some of the features of the duck— the long, oval body and head, curved neck, wide beak, small tail, variegated plumage.

Technique A thin layer of clay ($1/3$ inch) is spread over the bottom of the lid. The format is horizontal; a preliminary pencil sketch of the duck should fill the whole area. The pebbles are then set at regular intervals (width of a knitting needle) and pressed through to the cardboard. They must still stick out of the clay. Because of the limited color range, strong emphasis is given to the contrast of light and dark. The arrangement of the pebbles follows the shape of the body and the position of the feathers.

Flat stones are used for lines and areas; stones set on edge are used for dots. The background can be decorated; if left plain, it must be smoothed.

The plaster (for mixing see page 145) is carefully poured over the mosaic, filling the lid completely. Names are engraved on the back. After the plaster has set, lid and clay are carefully removed; the mosaic is left to dry for 24 hours. The finished mosaic is cleaned with the sponge. The process of setting is reversed for cement. We use cement and finely sifted sand instead of plaster. Cement and sand, mixed in equal proportions with water to a stiff consistency, are poured into a plywood frame or a very strong cardboard lid. The pebbles are arranged directly in the cement, so that we see the front of the mosaic. Cement sets slowly and therefore gives us ample time to complete the design.

To achieve more intense color effects the pebbles are finally waxed with floor polish. Cement as well as plaster can be dyed (see page 164).

Similar Subjects: monkey / blackbird / artist / bear / bunch of flowers / buffalo / dragon / lizard / elephant / donkey / owl / pheasant / spotted salamender / fish / heron / flamingo / frog / fox / goose / giraffe / cock / harlequin / witch / stag / chicken / dog / Indian / jaguar / beetle / camel / rabbit / cat / screech owl / crocodile / leopard / lion / ladybird / marabou / marten / mask / sea gull / marmot / rhinoceros / Neptune / hippopotamus / panther / parrot / peacock / horse / crow / bird of paradise / rider on horseback / boa constrictor / sheep / tortoise / snail / swan / pig / sea horse / bull / stork / dancer / pigeon / tiger / birds (G) / wood / ram / weasel / wolf / zebra / goat / circus (G) / zoo.

III. Clay, Porcelain, and Glass Mosaic. An Angel

Materials   Glass, pottery and porcelain fragments; possibly a glass cutter; box lid, about 12 inches by 8 inches and ³/₄ inch deep. Each child will also require between 3 and 4 pounds of plaster; a pencil; a piece of charcoal; possibly a pane of glass.

Subject   The lesson begins with a brief introductory talk. An angel can be shown in different attitudes (kneeling, standing, floating, etc.). He has wings, a long dress, long hair, and a halo.

Technique   Glass, pottery, and porcelain fragments, both plain and patterned, can be used. As an alternative, the children can dye small panes of glass and cut pieces of the required size and shape with the glass cutter. The glass, in this case, will be painted with undiluted poster color. It is cut, on the unpainted side, into strips between ¹/₂ inch and 1¹/₂ inches wide.

The glass can be set flat as well as upright. If the mosaic is set directly into the lid of the box, the pieces, to be attached with glue, can only be placed flat. In the case of a plaster cement or clay ground, an interplay of flat and upright portions should be aimed at.

The angel is drawn in outline into the cardboard or the plaster ground, using a knitting needle. The format can be vertical or horizontal; the figure should fill the entire area.

Glass dyed by the children is placed into the ground on the colored side. Gaps should be about ¹/₁₆ inch wide, so that each portion of mosaic is completely surrounded by plaster or cement, etc. Alternatively, the design can be drawn on a piece of paper over which a sheet of glass is placed. The mosaic (flat pieces only) is then arranged on the glass.

A wooden frame will be needed for pouring the plaster or cement mixture. For pouring, see page 135; for coloring plaster, see page 164.

Similar subjects: monkey / Ali Baba / ant / blackbird / artist / bunch of asters / bee / flowers / bunch of flowers / buffalo / clown / dahlia / David and Goliath / cathedral / Sleeping Beauty / dragon / lizard / jackdaw / duck / Eskimo / owl / fern / pheasant / fish / heron / flamingo / frog / fox / goose / goose girl / gardener / Puss in Boots / goldfish / harbor / cock / harlequin / witch / stag / shepherd and his flock (G) / wedding procession (G) / chicken / dog / hedgehog / Indian / insects / beetle / cat / screech owl / the three wise men from the East / crane / crab / crocodile / leopard / dragonfly / dandelion / ladybird / mask / ocean bed / soldiers / man in the moon / minster / nightingale / daffodil / Neptune / oasis / fruit picking / palace / parrot / bird of paradise / peacock / horse / prince / princess / crow / deer / rider on horseback / reindeer / boa constrictor / knight / Robinson Crusoe / Little Red Ridinghood / tortoise / snail / swallow / swimming / sea horse / tightrope-walker / sunflower / spider / Santa Claus / dance / pigeon / animals (G) / tiger / national costumes / wood / magic gardens / zebra / circus.

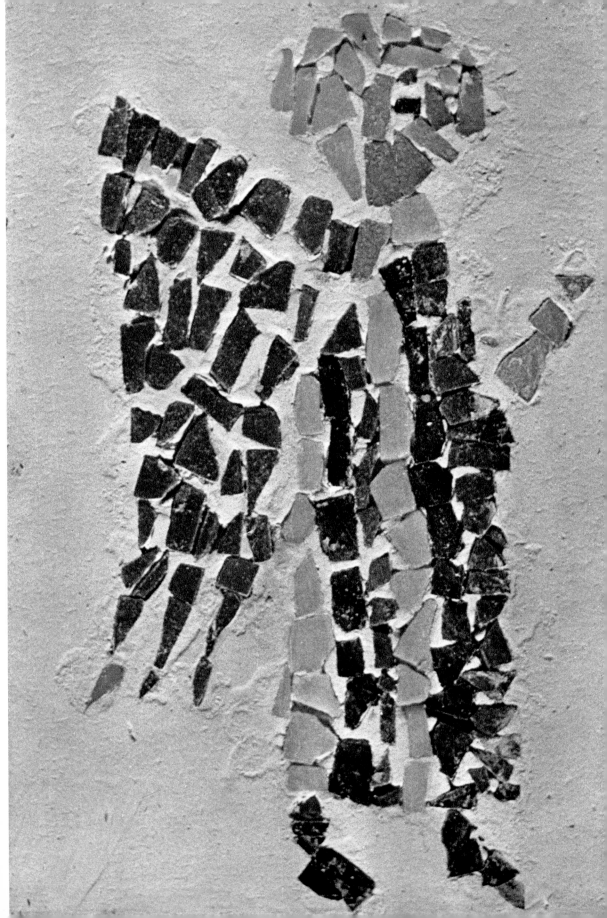

Illustrations for page 144

G. Plastic Techniques

Sculpture in the Round

Free-standing sculpture is described as sculpture in the round. Since it can be seen from different angles, its forms have to be worked out in every part. It is therefore important to choose subjects of a distinctly three-dimensional character.

The child will find it easier to build up sculpture piece by piece than to work it out of the mass. The second method demands a clear concept not only of the object itself, but also of the nature of the surrounding space.

Plasticine and Clay

Children will already have worked in clay and plasticine in the nursery. Plasticine (oil clay) does not smear or dry out and can therefore be used again and again. The technique should be introduced in the first grade. Since it is obtainable in every color, plasticine appeals greatly to smaller children. But since it is very expensive, clay is to be preferred for larger and more permanent work. It has to be kept free from foreign bodies.

Though it is worked as easily as plasticine, clay dries quickly and therefore has to be wrapped in wet rags. Once an object has dried, it cannot be modeled any further. In its unfired state, clay can be broken up, damped, re-kneaded, and used again. There is no better modeling tool than the hand. Other aids (spatula, knife, the handle of a spoon, etc.) are not used until later. The finished work has to dry for two to three weeks before firing; then it can be painted with pottery colors or possibly glazed (all over or in parts). Fired, unpainted clay turns brick red. Glazes can be matt, shiny, neutral (resembling a coating of glass), and colored. The glaze makes pottery waterproof. We should aim in modeling to distinguish between the convex and the concave curve, the billowing and the receding line. The hand constructs, while the mind seeks expression in plastic form. Modeling is of great help in developing the sense of touch, a feeling for shape, and an awareness of the space surrounding an object.

If clay cannot be obtained from a nearby pottery or brickworks, it can usually be bought through an art school, where the children's work will also be fired.

Clay Modeling I. A Witch

Materials   2 pounds of clay per pupil; spatula or spoon handle; base (hardboard, slate, etc.), about 8 inches by 8 inches.

Subject   For the subject, see page 65.

Technique   The children begin by working out the different blocks with their fingers. Having articulated the figure into a head block, a block for the body, etc., the detail is developed with fingers and spatula. There should be clear, plastic shapes, without, as far as possible, any grooves, hollows, or angles. Individual parts must be carefully joined (children tend to join them very loosely). Particular care must be taken over smaller sections (arms, head, eyes, nose, buttons).

There must be no air bubbles in the clay, if the figure is not to burst in the course of firing. Joins for arms, nose, and stick must extend over a wide area, care being taken that kneading is particularly thorough at these points. Very long and thin forms (arms, stick) should be made as part of the body rather than separately. The shoes disappear under the skirt or can be attached to the hem.

Finally, each separate portion is carefully beaten with the flat end of the spatula to free it from adhering crumbs of clay. This will also ensure a clean finish for each separate part.

Walls of clay more than 1 inch thick will burst in firing. The finished work will therefore have to be carefully hollowed out. To provide an air outlet, large shapes can be modeled over a core of silver paper (linked to the outside) which will melt in firing. When complete the figure must be separated from the base or it will crack in the course of drying.

Having dried, the figure can be finished (in parts only) with sandpaper. In painting with pottery colors, the contrast between light and dark should be strongly emphasised. Finally, the glaze is applied, possibly only over limited areas, and the work is fired.

The example shown was done in the first grade (six to seven years).

Similar Subjects: acrobat / Ali Baba / angler / artist / baker / pheasant / broom-maker / the Christ child / clown / lady / David and Goliath / village band / Sleeping Beauty (G) / angel / Eskimo / fisherman / the goose girl / pedlar / a gentleman / shepherd / bride and bridegroom / Indian / fun fair (G) / Joseph and Mary / chimney sweep / cook / the three wise men from the East (G) / teacher / rabbit (G) / man from Mars / the military / man in the moon / sheep / Neptune / pirate / prince / princess / robber / rider on horseback / giant / knight / Robinson Crusoe / Little Red Ridinghood / chessmen / Snow White and the Seven Dwarfs / self-portrait / soldiers / Santa Claus / sportsman / dancer / William Tell / devil / various national costumes (G) / Nativity crib (figures) / Weather Bureau / the goblins (G) / magician / gypsy / circus people / dwarf.

140

Clay Modeling II. A Horse

Materials   Same as in the previous exercise.

Subject   The lesson begins with a short introductory talk about the main features of the horse. Its neck is proudly arched. It has hooves, a mane and a long tail, and wears saddle and bridle.

Technique   The horse can be built up in sections or modeled out of a block about 8 inches by 6 inches by 3¼ inches. There should not be too much detail, and only the fingers should be employed in the early stages. Forelegs and hind legs form two blocks. If the lines of head and neck are as horizontal as possible, there will be less danger of their breaking off. Neck and shoulders should join on a broad base. If necessary, a ball of silver paper connected to the outside can be used as a core. Detail is worked out with the spatula. The forms, though not excessively elaborate, should be developed in some detail and carefully joined. Mane and tail can be grooved or incised, etc., to provide some contrast in texture.

Forelegs and hind legs can be linked by a clay base to give them better support.

All forms over 1 inch thick are carefully hollowed out by the teacher. In the case of the legs, this is done by inserting a pencil. The body, unless modeled over a silver paper core, should be hollowed out from below.

The work is again dried (for at least a week), possibly painted (unpainted clay turns brick red), glazed (possibly only in parts), and fired.

The example shown was done in the s e c o n d grade (seven to eight years).

Similar subjects: monkey / blackbird / bear / buffalo / dragon / squirrel / lizard / polar bear / elephant / duck / donkey / owl / pheasant / spotted salamander / frog / fox / goose / Puss in Boots / giraffe / cock / hamster / hare / stag / chicken / dog / camel / rabbit / cat / screech owl / crocodile / cow / leopard / lion / marten / mouse / knife rest / sea gull / marmot / rhinoceros / hippopotamus / Easter bunny / panther / peacock / deer / rider on horseback / reindeer / sheep / tortoise / snail / pig / the head of a hobbyhorse / bull / stork / pigeon / tiger / ram / weasel / wolf / zebra / goat / circus animals / zoo.

Clay Modeling III. Coiled Pottery: Beaker and Jug

It is desirable that children make some pottery for use at least once during the first four grades of their school life.

Materials   2 pounds of clay per pupil; modeling tool; base; pottery colors; brush; sandpaper.

Subject   The difference between coiled pottery, as practiced by primitive peoples, and pottery made on the wheel is briefly explained to the children.

Technique   For the beaker, long ropes of clay of even thickness are rolled out on the table. The base is formed by coiling these ropes until a diameter of about 2¹/₂ inches has been reached. In the case of taller objects, the coils should be pressed together closely at this stage.

In forming the sides, each spiral is slightly larger than the previous one. The beaker will require between eight and ten coils.

The coils are then smoothed out between thumb and index finger, care being taken to close all the gaps to avoid bubbles. The beaker is then left to dry.

In the case of the jug, first form the base as for the beaker. The coils are drawn in again after the widest portion of the walls have been reached. Unlike the beaker, the jug has a lip for pouring. The handle, formed of a flat, comparatively wide, strip (about 2¹/₂ inches long, under ¹/₂ inch wide, and ¹/₄ inch thick), is attached to the still wet jug with very wet clay. Drying will take between two and three weeks.

When completely dry, jug and beaker are finished carefully with sandpaper inside and out. Painting with pottery colors should be simple and vigorous. The children can also be shown sgraffito technique in this connection.

The inside of any vessel meant to hold water has to be glazed. Glazing of the outside can be left to the teacher's discretion. The dried and glazed vessels are then ready for firing.

The examples shown (on page 138) were done in the t h i r d grade (eight to nine years).

Similar Objects: ashtray / flower bowl / egg cup / candlesticks / vase.

Plaster

Plaster is a very suitable material for children's work. It is easily worked, extremely versatile, and homogenous.

Plaster is, above all, used for making casts. But it can also be used in its own right, either for modeling out of the slightly liquid mass or for carving out of the solid plaster block. Very thin, long, or flat forms are reinforced with a wire frame (see page 153).

Wet and dry plaster do not adhere to one another. If work is interrupted, the dried plaster will have to be thoroughly damped again.

In the lower grades, the teacher should mix the plaster herself. To mix, a plastic bucket—or, for very small quantities, half a rubber ball or a plastic beaker—is filled one-third with water. The plaster powder is then cast on the water gradually, without stirring, until a plaster hill rises above the surface of the water. Water and plaster are used in equal proportion.

Stirring is done by hand, lumps being broken up with the fingers. Plaster can be used even when its consistency is fairly thin. Alternatively, it can be left to harden a little. This will happen very quickly. According to the work, plaster is used in a thinner or thicker consistency. Work must proceed very fast.

However, if you wish to have the work proceed slowly, either with or without a wire frame, the hardening of the plaster will have to be delayed. This is done by adding a few drops of spirits of gum or a solution of boric acid (3 parts of water to 1 part of boric acid solution). Plaster is either poured into molds or worked before it hardens. Once hardened, it should not be worked any more.

Objects from which the plaster cast or mold is to be detached should be given a thin coating of liquid soap.

Bags of plaster must be stored in an absolutely dry place, preferably in a wooden box resting on a wooden base. The slightest degree of dampness causes plaster to set and therefore makes it useless.

Tools must be cleaned carefully immediately after use.

For dyeing plaster, see page 164.

Plaster Sculpture I. A Chicken

Materials   4 to 5 pounds of plaster per pupil; wooden, hardboard, or enamel base; plastic bucket; spirits of gum.

Subject   The lesson begins with a brief introductory talk. The chicken stands firmly on the ground. Its two legs support an oval body with two projections, the neck with head and comb, and the tail.

Technique   The chicken is built up from the plaster mass, following the same procedure as in clay modeling. For mixing the plaster (possibly with a few drops of spirits of gum), see page 145. The plaster must be added in small quantities.

The legs are treated as a solid base, the long claws being marked by incisions on the surface. The body is shaped as a ball with two domed projections, one for the neck and head, the other for the tail. After painting the chicken in watercolor or decorating it in sgraffito with colored plaster, allow it to dry thoroughly.

The example shown was done in the s e c o n d grade (seven to eight years).

Similar Subjects: monkey / blackbird / artist / ballet dancer / bear / buffalo / Tom Thumb / dragon / polar bear / squirrel / elephant / duck / donkey / owl / spotted salamander / frog / fox / goose / giraffe / cock / hamster / harlequin / a gentleman / witch / a flock of sheep (G) / dog / hedgehog / jaguar / rabbit / cat / screech owl / cook / crocodile / cow / leopard / lion / marten / man from Mars / mouse / sea gull / marmot / nightingale / rhinoceros / devil / Neptune / hippopotamus / panther / peacock / horse / crow / rider / sheep / tortoise / pig / tightrope-walker / sportsman / Santa Claus / bull / pigeon / tiger / cattle market (G) / birds / Cinderella the goblins (G) / ram / weasel / wolf / zebra / goat / circus (G) / zoo / dwarf.

Plaster Sculpture II. Reinforced Plaster Figure: A Fox

This rather complicated type of work is intended for children in the third and fourth grades.

Materials   Each pupil will require about 15 yards of galvanized wire; a pair of pliers; 4 pounds of plaster. In addition, a plastic bucket and some spirits of gum will be needed for the whole class.

Subject   The lesson begins with a brief introductory talk, pointing out the main features of the fox, who has a pointed nose, long pointed ears, a long body, and creeps along.

Technique   It is best to show the children how to form the wire frame, which will more or less follow the shape of the fox (four long legs, spine, head and body, tail, and ears).

The frame is then placed into the lid of a box, which should barely exceed the dimensions of the fox. The plaster mixture for the base is then poured into the lid to a thickness of slightly over 1 inch.

The plaster for the body is now mixed, adding a few drops of spirits of gum to slow down the drying process. The plaster mixture is then applied directly to the frame. The different parts of the fox must be formed slowly and carefully. Projecting parts should be broad at the joins and tapering at the ends. For further strengthening, pieces of coarse string can be wrapped round the wire.

For dyeing plaster, see page 164.

The fox can also be painted with thinly diluted poster colors and polished afterwards with coarse sandpaper. This will produce an interesting texture.

The example shown was done in the third grade (eight to nine years).

Similar Subjects: monkey / angler / artist / ballet dancer / buffalo / clown / demon / David and Goliath / dragon / lizard / angel / Eskimo / acrobat on bicycle / pheasant / heron / flamingo / frog / football player / goose / ghost / Puss in Boots / cock / harlequin / a gentleman / witch / stag / shepherd / bride and bridegroom / dog / Indian chief / Joseph and Mary / camel / the battle of the knights / cat / cook / the three wise men from the East / crane / crab / crocodile / teacher / leopard / lion / marten / man from Mars / the military (G) / sea gull / bird of paradise / peacock / horse / prince / princess / robber chief / deer / reindeer / knight / Robinson Crusoe / tightrope-walker / self-portrait / skier / spider / sportsman / stork / dancer / devil / tiger / man and woman in national costumes / gymnast / monster / scarecrow / competitor / the goblins / ram / weasel / magic gardens / magician / zebra / goat / gypsy / circus people / zoo / dwarf.

Plaster Sculpture III. Plaster Carving: A Dog

Carving out of a block (plaster or wood) presupposes a strong imagination. It is most likely to be successful if the object in question is first drawn in outline on the sides of the block. Work of this kind is suitable for children in the fourth grade.

Materials Each pupil will require 2 pounds of plaster; box measuring about 6 inches by 4 inches by 2 inches; knife; some sandpaper. In addition, a plastic bucket, an assortment of files, and a chisel will be needed for the whole class.

Subject The lesson begins with a short introductory talk describing the main features of the dog.

Technique For making a plaster block, see pages 118 and 145. The mold, in this case, is the box, into which the plaster mixture is poured. In pouring, the sides of the different boxes act as supports. When the plaster has set, though not yet hardened, the cardboard has to be detached. If the plaster has become too dry, it can be made more workable again by immersing in water. The block is placed lengthwise on the base, and the dog is incised on it in outline with a nail, the utmost advantage being taken of the size of the block. This outline drawing should be slightly larger than the intended object. The surplus mass is then carved away immediately. The result will be an object not unlike a silhouette several inches thick. The edges are then cut into and the detail worked out, always bearing in mind that a carving should retain a slightly angular character.

The ears will appear as two small projections, either at the sides or the top of the head. The eyes will appear as two hemispheres or holes. Each pair of legs should form a block, divided only by a shallow cut. The paws project slightly. If the tail is meant to be long, its shape must be scraped out of the plaster with considerable care. The coat can be slightly stippled or grooved. If necessary, some of the surfaces can be smoothed with sandpaper, although not to such a degree that the character of the carving suffers.

The example shown was done in the fourth grade (nine to ten years).

Similar Subjects: monkey / Noah's ark / bear / well / buffalo / squirrel / duck / Eskimo / owl / fish / frog / fox / goose / cock / hamster / hare / house / a witch's house / skyscraper / chicken / hut / camel / rabbit / cat / screech owl / church / crocodile / cow / leopard / lion / marten / mask / mouse / marmot / rhinoceros / hippopotamus / panther / horse / boa constrictor / sheep / palace / pig / bull / pigeon / tiger / the goblins / weasel / windmill / wolf / dream house / goat / zoo (G) / dwarf.

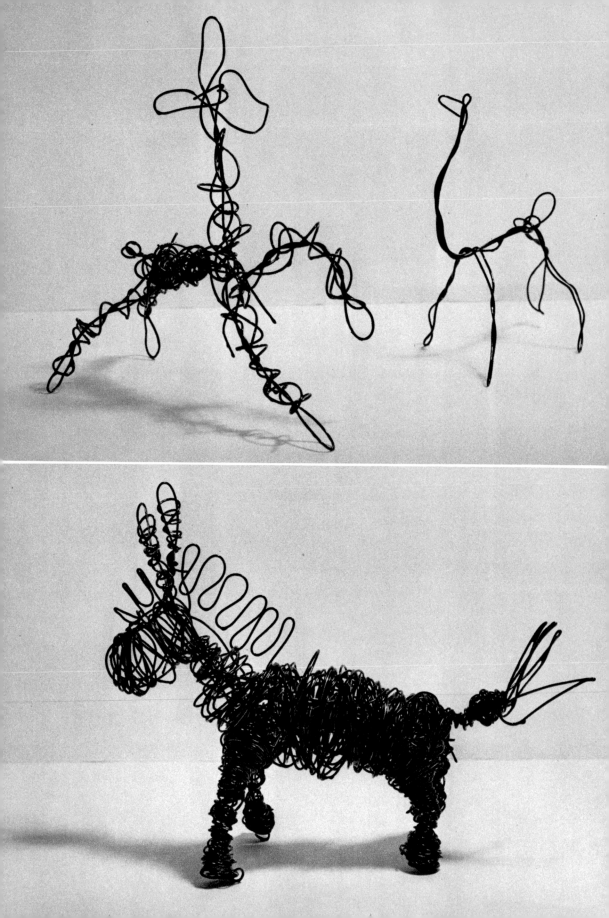

Wire

Flexible wire is suitable both for the making of sculpture in the round and for two-dimensional objects.

All we need is galvanized wire of different gauges. Principal tools are the fingers, possibly aided by flat-nosed pliers. If colored wires, such as those used by electricians are not available, the work can be finished with colored lacquer.

It is important to choose subjects that lend themselves to this technique.

Wire Sculpture I. Linear and Coiled Wire Sculpture: A Donkey

Materials Each pupil will require 18 feet of highly flexible wire (galvanized and possibly of several gauges), or pieces of colored electrician's wire; flat-nosed and pointed pliers. The teacher should also have a supply of lacquer, a brush, and some turpentine or turps substitute.

Subject The lesson begins with a brief introductory talk, pointing out the main features of the donkey, who has a large head, long ears, arched neck, a mane, a tasseled tail, and hooves like a horse.

Technique 1. Linear Wire Sculpture
The children try to form a donkey in one line (see illustration), beginning with the underside. The legs are formed by four loops; the tail consists of a short loop; head, neck, and ears of a long one. This is an excellent opportunity for experimenting in drawing out and joining wire. Wire is particularly suitable for mobiles, which are hung up on a thin thread.
2. Coiled Wire Sculpture
We first form a kind of skeleton (similar to linear wire sculpture) and then wind the separate portions with wire according to their shape and thickness. The tassel of the tail, mane, and ears can be formed in simple loops.
The children should be shown how to prevent the wire coils from slipping off (by loops or knots), particularly where legs, tail, and ears join.
A prancing animal, supported by three legs only, will stand more securely than one on all fours. Wire can be painted with black or white metal paint. The paint should be slightly diluted with turps or turps substitute.

The example shown was done in the second grade (seven to eight years).

Similar Subjects: Linear wire sculpture (as if outlined with a pencil): clown / demon / thistle / lizard / fish / pheasant / heron / goose / ghost / giraffe / stag / harlequin / grasshopper / dog / camel / cathedral / crane / runner / leopard / man from Mars / nightingale / panther / peacock / cyclist / deer / reindeer / spider / stork / dancer / pigeon / devil / weasel / goat / dwarf.
Mobiles (swimming, hovering, flying): bee / demon / bat / flamingo / airplane / ghost / bumblebee / beetle / dragonfly / sea gull / parrot / bird of paradise / butterfly / swallow / sea horse / bird.
Coiled wire sculpture: ant / blackbird / angler / bee / buffalo / clown / dragon / lizard / ice hockey player / flamingo / airplane / fox / goose / cock / hedgehog / centaur / crab / crocodile / lion / marten / mouse / marmot / rhinoceros / crow / caterpillar / sheep / tortoise / bull / goat / dwarf.

Wire Sculpture II. Wire Wound with Raffia: A Giraffe

Wire sculpture wound with raffia can be attempted in the fourth grade (nine to ten years). Younger children generally find this type of work too difficult.

Materials Every pupil will require about 2 yards of flexible galvanized wire; some rags; some cotton wool. In addition strands of raffia of different colors will be needed for the whole class.

Subject The lesson begins with a short introductory talk pointing out the main features of the giraffe, an animal with a long neck, small ears, and short stubby horns. Its body rests diagonally on a pair of long forelegs and somewhat shorter hind legs. It also has a comparatively short tail and split hooves.

Technique The giraffe is formed in twisted wire without any special preparation. Twisting the wire—with a pencil—gives it extra strength. Care must be taken to form loops at points of intersection. The remains of the wire are wound round the frame. At the ends (legs, horns, ears, tail), the wire loop should be left open, so that the raffia can be tied up at these points.

The frame is padded with bits of wool and cotton wool; it is important to pack and wind very closely.

Finally, each pupil chooses two colors from the skeins of different-colored raffia. The raffia should be spread out before winding begins. Winding should start at the extremities, where the raffia is tied on. The raffia should be crossed frequently, and tied from time to time. Care should be taken to achieve an effect of plasticity.

Depending on the subject, colors can be used together or separately.

The example shown was done in the fourth grade (nine to ten years).

Similar Subjects: artist / ballet (G) / bee / flowers / buffalo / chameleon / thistle / dragon / lizard / donkey / Eskimo / pheasant / spotted salamander / flamingo / cock / harlequin / hare / grasshopper / stag / bride and bridegroom / chicken / dog / bumblebee / Indian / insects / beetle / cat / screech owl / crane / crocodile / dragonfly / lion / ladybird / mouse / sea gull / nightingale / Cinderella / parrot / bird of paradise / peacock / robber / reindeer / boa constrictor / sheep / swallow / spider / sportsman / bull / stork / dancer / devil / tiger / man and woman in national costumes / birds / wild animals / ram / weasel / wolf / zebra / goat / dwarf.

Wood

Because of its hardness, wood makes heavy demands on the strength and perseverance of the children. Carving out of the block (sculpture in the round) or the board (relief) should first be attempted in a soft wood like lime, using a sharp knife. It is not really suitable for children under ten or eleven.

Sculpture in roots, branches, or fir cones, gathered by the children, can, however, be attempted at any age. The material itself suggests the subject.

Root Sculpture

Materials Roots and branches of every kind of tree. The most interesting shapes are those of the vine. The only requirements are a sharp knife, a drill, and some cold glue.

Subject and Technique Most roots and branches contain the suggestion of some kind of figure. To develop this hidden form is the task of the lesson. The most important tool is the penknife. Very thin twigs can be glued into previously drilled holes. Any natural roughness of the surface is left untouched.

The examples shown were done in the fourth grade (nine to ten years).

Similar Subjects: demon / dragon / lizard / spotted salamander / ghost / witch / hedgehog / beetle / crocodile / marten / mask / mouse / lake dwelling / snake / snail / dancer / devil / monster / weasel / dwarf.

Paper

Paper can not only be drawn on, painted, and printed; it can also be torn, pasted together, folded, and used for all kinds of sculpture. Soaked, it can be turned into papier-mâché, a material highly suitable for modeling. As it is very cheap, it is ideal for use in schools.

Paper Sculpture I. Puppet Heads in Papier-Mâché

Materials Newspaper; wallpaper paste; poster colors; sponge; palette; water bowl; brush; colorless varnish; bucket.

Subject The character of a puppet must be obvious at once. Shape and color are therefore accentuated to produce a certain type, for puppets always represent types with unvarying attributes. The king has white hair, a crown, a furrowed brow, and an aquiline nose. The devil looks evil, has a curved nose, thin lips, pointed ears, arched eyebrows, and horns. Punch has an honest face, though he is not without cunning. The fairy princess has beautiful long hair and gentle features, while the witch is thin and ugly, with a single tooth in her enormous mouth.

Technique Papier-mâché is made by soaking torn-up newspapers overnight in a bucket of wallpaper paste. In the case of heavily glued paper, water alone is sufficient. The pulpy mass has to be thoroughly kneaded until all the paste is absorbed.

The head should be between 2½ and 3½ inches high, the neck between 1 inch and 2½ inches long.

The teacher shows the children how to form the head by wrapping several pieces of dry newspaper over the end of a cardboard tube. Then the papier-mâché is applied over the dry core, until the head is roughly the size of a tennis ball. Eyes, nose, chin, etc., are then modeled out of the round. Details, such as lips, ears, the single tooth of the witch, cheeks (fat or hollow), and even hat or crown, should be worked out very distinctly.

Finally, the uppermost layer of papier-mâché is smoothed down and the head left to dry.

Alternatively, we can use a mixture of wallpaper paste, sawdust, and newsprint in equal parts. This mass is again thoroughly kneaded and applied over the dry paper core. It is then worked like papier-mâché, except that very thin and delicate forms will have to be reinforced with wire. All puppets must have a ridge at the base of the neck for attaching their clothes.

The finished heads are painted with poster colors, aiming at vigorous, contrasting effects. To achieve a light complexion, a base of flake white can be used. Finally, the painted heads are given a coat of clear varnish for protection. Beards, wigs, crowns, etc., are added afterwards. The hands—again over cardboard tubes to allow the player to operate them—are kneaded of the same mass as the heads. They should indicate only the simplest gestures.

The example shown was done in the second grade (seven to eight years).

Similar subjects: monkey / artist / bear / buffalo / clown / lady / Tom Thumb / dragon / squirrel / polar bear / elephant / angel / duck / donkey / owl / frog / fox / gardener / Puss in Boots / cock / harlequin / a gentleman / witch / shepherd / chicken / dog / fun fair (G) / chimney sweep / screech owl / cook / miner / teacher / rabble (G) mask / rhinoceros / mouse / Neptune / hippopotamus / horse / pirate / robber / rider on horseback / giant / knight / pig / bull / panther / devil / birds / the goblins / weasel / magician / zebra / goat / dwarf.

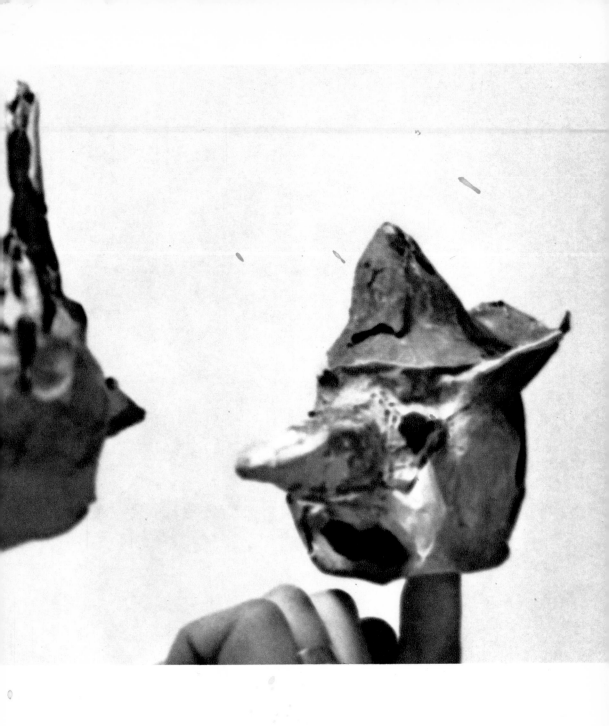

Paper Sculpture II. Masks from Paper Bags and Cardboard Boxes

It would be too difficult for younger children to model paper masks in papier-mâché. We choose a simpler method and use paper bags and cardboard boxes.

Materials   Large paper bags or cardboard boxes; scraps of wool or odd bits of material; glue; scissors; feathers; poster colors; sponge, palette; brush; water bowl; colorless varnish.

Technique   1. Masks from Paper Bags
Large paper bags can be put over the head. The face (eyes, cheeks, warts, furrows, teeth, lips) is painted, aiming at contrasting effects and simple forms. A coating of colorless varnish acts as protection against dampness. The openings for eyes and mouth are not cut out until the end. The nose can be put on. Beards, tusks, eyebrows, and hair can be made from scraps of paper, wool, or raffia.
2. Masks from Cardboard Boxes
Neck, nose, mouth, and openings for the eyes have to be fitted in the appropriate places. Nose, teeth, tongue, etc., can be stuck on. Finally, the grotesquely painted mask is given a coating of colorless varnish.

The example shown was done in the second grade (seven to eight years).

Paper Sculpture III. A Fish

Paper cutting and folding is related to other techniques (folding cut, silhouette, etc.). But unlike these, it makes use of the plastic potentialities of paper. Paper can be bent, rolled, folded, etc. All these possibilities are also inherent in metal foil.

Materials Every pupil will require a sheet of corrugated paper (possibly colored by the children), about 12 inches by 8 inches; stiff white paper of different textures; knitting needle; pencil; scissors; razor blade or cutting pen.

Technique First the shape of the fish is cut out in white paper (about 10 inches long). Having been cut out, the fish is placed against the colored corrugated paper. The form of the fish should be outlined on the paper in colored pencil. Narrow strips of white paper are then inserted through slits in the corrugated base to represent waves.

Scales and fins are similarly made by cutting into the fish and inserting strips of different colored, slightly stiff paper, or by cutting into the fish and folding the paper back (see illustration). The fish is fastened to its corrugated paper base by being cut into in three places (8) and by drawing the resultant strips to the back of the corrugated paper, where they are pasted down.

Similar Subjects: Noah's ark / automobile / dredger / bridge / castle / buffalo / clown / steamship / dragon / railway / elephant / owl / factory / pheasant / airplane / fox / goose / cock / harlequin / bookbinding / a witch's house / hedgehog / cathedral / lion / machine / mask / palace / parrot / peacock / knight / sheep / sea horse / sportsman / Santa Claus / birds of all kinds / ram / windmill / zebra.

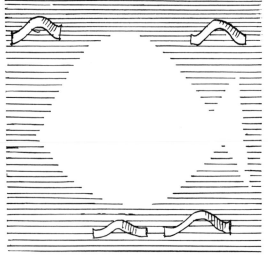
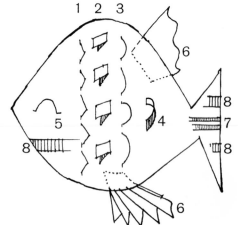

Relief

A relief is sculpture confined to the plane.

To children, the transition from two-dimensional drawing to drawing on a plaster or clay base is but a small step. Many relief techniques are therefore already suitable for younger children. The child draws in outline in the clay. The next stage involves removing the substance between the lines. This demands less imagination than positive modeling. The child prefers to scratch out and to remove—*i.e.*, he models in the negative; this would also appear to be the more natural process.

Subjects should be of a linear and two-dimensional character.

Relief I. Plaster Graffito and Plaster Relief

See Plaster engraving, page 118.

Materials Every pupil will require from 3 to 4 pounds of plaster; cardboard box (about 12 inches by 10 inches); a knife, knitting needle, or nail. In addition, the teacher will need a plastic bucket for mixing.

Technique Plaster graffito and plaster relief are closely related to drawing. Plaster graffito is limited chiefly to the scratching and cutting of lines (see page 118). Whole areas can be scraped out in the same manner. The result is a kind of negative (similar to the silhouette) which can be used for printing (see page 118); this is known as a plaster intaglio. Areas can be scraped out to any depth, until the result is an object in almost full sculpture, where there may even be some undercutting. In the fourth grade (nine to ten years), soft slate can be used instead of plaster.

Relief II. Plaster Sgraffito: A Dragon

Every sgraffito is a bas-relief. Two layers of plaster of different colors are poured into the lid of a box. The first layer is left to dry, though it has to be damped again before pouring the second layer, which is allowed to harden sufficiently to be scraped without difficulty. Through scraping (*i.e.*, sgraffito), the first layer is partly revealed. The result is a colored sgraffito. Plaster sgraffito is suitable for children from the second grade (seven to eight years).

Materials   Same as in Plaster Relief I. In addition, the teacher will need two buckets and powder paints soluble in water.

Subject   The lesson begins with a short introductory talk. A dragon is like a giant lizard with an enormous mouth, sharp teeth, one or several poisonous tongues, nostrils emitting fire, claws, a long crested tail, and wings.

Technique   The technique is entirely two-dimensional. The dragon is cut out of the cardboard.

For dyeing the plaster, we can use fast powder colors soluble in water, tempera colors (in tubes), or possibly ink or brick dust. Aniline dyes are not satisfactory. The colors, thickly mixed with water, are added to the plaster mixture, which has been carefully prepared as described. It is necessary to work fast, before the plaster has a chance to set. The white plaster mixture is then poured into the lid of the box to a thickness of slightly under $1/2$ inch and left to dry. A second, colored, layer is then poured in, though only to a thickness of about $1/16$ inch. This layer is not allowed to dry completely, so that it does not offer too much resistance to the scraping tool. The outline of the cardboard dragon is traced lightly with a nail. Then the first layer is penetrated, and the figure is either scraped out (negative, or intaglio), or the surrounding area is removed (relief).

Two holes are carefully made at the back, so that the finished work can be hung on the wall over two nails.

Sgraffito is also widely used in the ceramic arts.

The example shown was done in the s e c o n d grade (seven to eight years).

Similar Subjects: monkey / blackbird / artist / people bathing / ballet dancer / bear / buffalo / clown / chameleon / cathedral / lizard / jackdaw / angel / owl / trick cyclist / fern / pheasant / spotted salamander / fish / heron / flamingo / bat / frog / fox / goose / Puss in Boots / cock / harlequin / witch / stag / chicken / dog / Indian / jaguar / beetle / camel / cat / centaur / crane / crab / crocodile / cow / runner / leopard / dragonfly / lion / dandelion / ladybird / marten / mask / sea gull / marmot / rhinoceros / native dance / Neptune / hippopotamus / panther / bird of paradise / peacock / horse racing / deer / rider on horseback / reindeer / boa constrictor / knight / sheep / tortoise / snail / swallows / swans / swimmer / sea horse / sunflower / spider / sportsman / bull / stork / dance / pigeon / tiger / bird / competitor / ram / weasel / wolf / zebra / goat.

Relief III. Plaster Relief from a Plasticine or Clay Negative:
Christmas Tree or Sailing Ship

Forms modeled in intaglio in plasticine or clay, or cut into linoleum, can be cast in plaster. Plasticine will be used for smaller, clay for larger, reliefs.

Materials   Every pupil will require about 2 pounds of plaster, plasticine, or clay; spatula; knitting needle; pencil; 2 or 3 long strips of cardboard (about 1¼ inches wide) or the lid of a cardboard box (12 inches by 8 inches). The teacher will need a plastic bucket for mixing the plaster.

Subject   The lesson begins with a short introductory talk. A Christmas tree has a thick trunk, thin branches and twigs, candles, and Christmas decorations. A sailing ship has powerfully curved bows, rigging, etc.

Technique   1. Christmas Tree (modeled in plasticine)

The plasticine is first put into a square, oval, or round box. It is then smoothed to form a slab. The negative forms are carefully worked into the plasticine, first with fingers, then with the spatula, nail, or pencil, the plasticine being deeply cut into for the tree trunk, less deeply for the branches, and only superficially for the needles. Every line should be V-shaped in cross section. The apples on the tree are pressed in with the fingers. Any plasticine scraped out is carefully put aside. Finally, the relief is coated with liquid soap and surrounded by the cardboard strips, whose ends must overlap.

Alternatively, the relief can be made directly in the lid of a box. For making a cast, see page 145. Several casts are possible, provided the mold is coated in liquid soap each time.

When the plaster has set, the cardboard strips are removed and the plasticine relief is detached. We have then obtained a plaster positive, which, having been allowed to dry completely, is cleaned with a sponge.

If the final cast is sponged in color and polished afterwards with sandpaper, the result will be a light tree against a dark background. Relief slabs which have cracked can be joined at the back with another layer of plaster.

The example shown was done in the first grade (six to seven years).

2. A Sailing Ship

The children require a flat, firm base of glass, cardboard, etc., covered with a sheet of plastic. The clay, smooth and carefully kneaded, should form a slab slightly under 1 inch thick, measuring about 10 inches by 7^1/$_4$ inches. Forms of varying depths are worked out with fingers, knife, and knitting needle. The bows of the ship are deepest, next come the masts and sails, then ropes, ladders, flags, etc. The initials on sails and life boats must be carved in reverse. Before casting and making the mold (as for the previous example), surfaces are smoothed again.

3. Linocuts

Casts can also be made from linocuts. The result will be a plaster negative. For making these casts, the linocut is best placed into a fitting cardboard lid.

4. Clay Reliefs from a Plaster Negative

The whole process can also be reversed. We make a plaster negative, press the clay against it to a thickness of between ^{1}/$_2$ inch and 1 inch, and carefully lift off the resulting clay relief, which, having dried, can be painted, glazed, and fired.

The example shown was done in the first grade (six to seven years).

Similar Subjects: monkey / ant / blackbird / artist / automobile / people bathing / ballet dancer / bear / bee / flowers / botanical gardens / buffalo / chameleon / clown / David and Goliath / cathedral / village / village band / dragon / squirrel / lizard / railway / ice hockey player / polar bear / elephant / angel / duck / donkey / Eskimo / owl / factory / cyclist / fern / pheasant / fish / heron / flamingo / bat / frog / football / goose / goose girl / gardener / Puss in Boots / gondola / city / cock / harlequin / hare / herd / witch / stag / shepherd / wedding / chicken / dog / hedgehog / Indian / insects / the hunt / jaguar / beetle / cage with animals / camel / fight (knights, Red Indians, animals) / sports competition / cat / screech owl / centaur / the three wise men from the East / crane / crab / crocodile / cow / a drive in a coach / runner / leopard/ dragonfly / favorite occupation / lion / dandelion / locomotive / market day / marten / man from Mars / mask / the military / sea gull / church / marmot / rhinoceros / native dance / Neptune / hippopotamus / fruit-picking / palace / desert island / panther / parrot / peacock / horse / prince / princess / crow / racing cyclist / the Pied Piper / of Hamelin / deer / rider / reindeer / knight / Robinson Crusoe / sheep / tortoise / snake / tobogganing / snail / Snow White and the Seven Dwarfs / story of creation / educational trip / flight of swallows / swan / pig / swimmer / sea horse / tightrope-walker / skier / soldiers / sunflower / spider / sportsman / Santa Claus / town / walking on stilts / bull / stork / on the beach / storm / fir tree / dance / pigeon / William Tell / devil / tiger / jungle.

Relief IV. Wire Relief: Tower of Babel or Magic Garden

Flexible wire is a most rewarding material. All kinds of forms can be made from it, both two- and three-dimensional.

Materials   Every pupil will require between 8 and 10 yards of galvanized wire of different gauges; flat-nosed and pointed pliers; deal board about 12 inches to 10 inches, painted dark or light in poster color. The teacher will also need several old brushes, black or white paint, and a few hammers.

Subject   The lesson begins with a brief introductory talk. The Magic Garden is full of strange flowers, fruits, and plants. The children make all kinds of shapes and ornaments, which, placed next to and above each other, are joined into a garden.

For the Tower of Babel, several structural components are made. These, joined above and next to each other, form a modern Tower of Babel. The tower must rise into the sky. Everybody builds his own tower of parts freely invented by him.

Technique   The aim is a rhythmic play of line. The children are shown the enormous range of forms which can be achieved with wire. The different pieces of wire should measure between 4 and 8 inches. None should exceed 12 inches (the length of the base).

Wire can be painted, in the case of a dark ground—white; on a light ground—black.

The different components are attached with small staples. For the Magic Garden, the format can be vertical or horizontal; for the Tower of Babel it must be vertical. The Magic Garden can be laid out quite freely, while the Tower of Babel requires some planning in regard to proportions, etc. Two or more joined parts must produce new forms.

If some soldering equipment is available, the different forms will be soldered together before being lacquered and attached to their base.

The finished work is hung up by a cord, which passes through two staples.

The example shown was done in the fourth grade (nine to ten years).

Similar Subjects: switchback / monkey / ant / aquarium (G) / artist / automobiles / dredger / station / ballet (G) / bee / slowworm / flower garden / botanical gardens / herd of buffalo / clown / dahlia / steamship / thistle / cathedral / village / village band / dragon / lizard / railway / elephants in the jungle / angel / owl / factory / trick cyclist / fern / pheasant / fisherman / fishing port / heron / flamingo / bat / airplane / fox / football player / galley / ghost / herd of giraffe (G) / journey in a gondola / harbor / cock / herd / leaping stag / chicken / dog racing / Red Indian / imaginary insects / fun fair (G) / beetle / animals in a cage / camel / battle of the knights / cathedral / cat / screech owl / ceramics / the three wise men from the East / crane / crab / crocodile / runner / leopard / dragonfly / lion / man from Mars / machine / ocean bed / soldiers (G) / sea gulls in flight / church / native dance / Neptune / oasis / orchestra / palace / paradise / peacock / cycle racing / boa constrictor / Robinson Crusoe / sleigh ride / butterflies / snail / snowflakes / flight of swallows / swans / swimmer / sea horse / sailboat / tightrope-walker / spider / sportsman / town / bullfight / stork / fir tree / dance / pigeon / tiger / dream / gymnast / jungle / birds / wood / Cinderella / ram / weasel / windmill / skyscraper / robot / dream house / magician / magic gardens / tent / goat / circus.

Relief V. Wire Jewelry

Here, flexible wire is used to make simple jewelry.

Materials Each pupil will require 3 feet of copper or brass wire; flat-nosed and pointed pliers; knitting needle; pencil.

Technique The children are shown how to make simple decorative forms such as curved lines, loops, spirals, etc.

It must be possible to join separate forms without soldering. Ends must be finished carefully if they are not to scratch. Links should be as small as possible; they can be made by rolling the wire over a knitting needle.

Suitable objects are necklaces, brooches, pendants, chaplets, bracelets, or rings.

Only two or three simple motifs should be used for a chain. These should be repeated on the same or different scale, or combined in brass and copper. The children should be encouraged to experiment with grouping and spacing. Where necessary, pieces can be soldered.

Wire jewelry might be made as a Christmas assignment in the third or fourth grades.